Two Minutes for Talking to Myself

By Curt Keilback

 FriesenPress

One Printers Way
Altona, MB R0G 0B0
Canada

www.friesenpress.com

Forward: Paul MacLean
Illustrator: Warren Keilback
w.keilback1@gmail.com

ISBN
978-1-03-914600-6 (Hardcover)
978-1-03-914599-3 (Paperback)
978-1-03-914601-3 (eBook)

1. Biography & Autobiography, Sports

Distributed to the trade by The Ingram Book Company

Table of Contents

Part 2

Part 3

Part 4

Part 5

Acknowledgements

FIRST OFF, THANK YOU Paul MacLean for writing the fore-word. You've always been a class act!

Thank you to the many coaches, managers, and players I had the privilege to deal with over the better part of three decades.

Thank you to my fellow broadcasters, writers, show hosts, public relations people, producers and directors, operators, and everybody behind the scenes.

Thank you, Geoff Kirbyson, author of *THE HOTLINE* and *BROKEN RIBS AND POPCORN* for your promotional advice.

Thank you, hockey fans, for all the kind words over the years.

And most of all, thank you family for putting up with my prolonged winter absences, especially over those early years in Phoenix.

Most of what you'll read is positive, even funny, but I did grind an axe in one of the later stories. (It was good for my soul.)

Foreword

I WAS REALLY PLEASED when Curt asked me to write the foreword for his book *Two Minutes for Talking to Myself*. The time he has been involved with the Winnipeg Jets through to the days in Phoenix gives him the perspective that no one else has. Curt was involved with owners, general managers, business executives, coaches, equipment, medical staff, and the players. He knew these people on a daily basis and learned about them all.

This book is a comprehensive look at the people that made up the Winnipeg Jets/Phoenix Coyotes over the years. Curt brings out the characters that they were and what it was like to be a part of the growth of the NHL thru the merger with the WHA.

This book has insights on owners like Barry Shenkarow to executives Mike Smith and Fergie. Friar Nicolson, his mentor and partner; Coaches Tom McVie and Tom Watt and players; The Golden Jet, Ducky, Kitty, Buzzard, Babs, Coma, Repo, and the Finnish Flash are all in the book somewhere.

What I like the most about the book is that it gives the fans a look at how much fun it was to be an NHL player in the '80s and '90s when the league expanded. This was when travel was commercial flights, first flight out day after games, and how much time the Jets spent at Minneapolis Airport; it was our second home. The fun we had waiting for flights, from getting seats together for card games to seniority for window or aisle seats with rookies in the middle.

I hope you enjoy reading this book as much as I did as it brought back many memories of my time with the Winnipeg Jets/ Phoenix Coyotes.

Congratulations to Sod; it's a five-minute penalty!

All the best, Big Mac.

This is a collection of short stories about hockey and broadcasting. I talk about the good days and the bad, fully aware that a bad day behind the mic at a hockey game is a good day anywhere else.

I hope you enjoy reading it as much as I enjoyed living it!

Curt Keilback spent seventeen years in the broadcast booth of the Winnipeg Jets and ten years calling games for the Coyotes in Phoenix. He also appeared in four hockey-themed movies, including *Goon* and *Goon 2*. These are his stories and opinions.

In the Beginning

THE CROWD AT THE Winnipeg Arena was in fever pitch as the final seconds ticked off, then nearly blew the walls down at the buzzer. The broadcasters managed to exclaim, "The Winnipeg Warriors have won the Edinburgh Cup!" before they were drowned out by the euphoria. It was all anybody heard on the radio for eight minutes. The broadcasters, Cactus Jack Wells and the guy he called "Kid," Jim Keilback, just sat back and let it all soak in, but they weren't alone. A wide-eyed seven-year-old was with them in the booth that night. I believe that was the moment I decided to be a hockey broadcaster when I grew up, just like my dad and his broadcast buddy, the late Cactus Jack Wells.

Years later, after a move from Winnipeg to Saskatchewan, my dream began to take shape; I broadcast senior hockey for the Yorkton Terriers. It continued in Regina, where I did play-by-play for the Pats team that won the Memorial Cup in 1974.

Later that year, I moved into television in Yorkton and presumed my days of doing play-by-play were over. But then, five years later came a phone call from a man I'd never met. Ken "Friar" Nicolson asked if I might consider joining him in the broadcast booth for Winnipeg Jet games. The Jets had just joined the NHL. I was beyond excited but did manage to ask, "How did you come by my name?" Nicolson replied, "Cactus Jack Wells recommended you. He said, 'Get the Kid's kid. He's in Saskatchewan.'"

In October 1979, I sat exactly where Cactus had been seated twenty-three years earlier. The circle was complete.

Thank you, Cactus. (You too, Kid.)

Debut

I STARTED IN RADIO when I was thirteen years old. I had a weekly show called *Minor Sports Corner* where I would pass on the results of the past week's little league games in Yorkton and area. I had ten minutes, but I was generally done in three. Apparently, I didn't have as much to say back then. A few years later, I was hired by the same station to do baseball play-by-play for the Yorkton Cardinals and the Melville Millionaires. They paid me five dollars a game. It was great!

Two years later, I got into radio on a full-time basis, again at CJ GX in Yorkton. My first salaried shift ($275/mo.) was as an evening disc jockey. However, I broke two of the three turntables that first night, and management decided that I would be of less harm in the newsroom.

I was given the title of "sports director" shortly after. What that really meant is that I was the only person in the department. I immediately became the voice of the Yorkton Terriers who won the Saskatchewan Senior league hockey championship. After two years there, I went to Regina where I did radio and television, but my favourite part of the job was play-by-play of the junior Rams of football and the Pats of junior hockey. Both those teams won Canadian championships. Little did I know that I would never again be the voice of a league champion.

CURT KEILBACK

The
New Voice
of the
Terriers

Follow the Terriers with Curt Keilback throughout the 1971-72 season . . . play-by-play descriptions of all home and away games, plus sportcasts at 8:10 a.m., 12:40 and 6:10 p.m. daily for the latest developments between games.

● GX 94 reports on sports at a Quarter To The Hour Every Hour.

GX RADIO 94

Yorkton Broadcasting Company Limited

Kill the Beast!

THE TERMS OF ENTRY to the NHL from the WHA were punitive. It wasn't a merger of the two leagues as much as a hostile takeover. The NHL wanted the WHA to die, and this was a way to ensure it. Each of the new teams (Winnipeg Jets, Edmonton Oilers, Quebec Nordiques, and Hartford Whalers) was allowed to protect four of their WHA players, including two goalies. That was it for top drawer talent. They had to fill the remaining roster spots with players who'd been passed over by the other seventeen NHL teams. Even at the draft, the WHA refugees were given the final four picks.

Prior to the season, Jets coach Tom McVie looked at his assistant Bill Sutherland and growled, "Sudsy, if we win ten games with this bunch, they should put us in the Hall of Fame."

Well, they won twenty, including one they really didn't want.

No Time Like the First Time

THE WINNIPEG JETS' FIRST year was like no other. There were no expectations; there could be no disappointments. The fans were just happy to have a team. Tens of thousands of people who'd been NHL fans from afar now had the opportunity to witness the real thing in their back yard.

The Jets were severely shortchanged in talent but big on work ethic. The fans loved it. For the players it was surreal; some had been convinced they'd never be in "the show," now they were not only in the NHL but local heroes. People like Lorne Stamler, Al Cameron, and Barry Melrose were recognized wherever they went. They were the subjects of local newspaper articles, of talk shows, and occasionally on a Saturday night, they even got to appear on *Hockey Night in Canada*! With the help of that unbridled enthusiasm, the first-year Jets went on to win twenty of their eighty games. It was quite an achievement, oddly too much achievement.

In those days, the NHL draft procedure was simple. If you finish at the bottom, you pick from the top; there was no draft lottery as there is now. Well, that year, Don Cherry's Colorado Rockies were every bit as bad a team as the Winnipeg Jets. The two clubs were tied for the last spot and, as fate would have it, they met on the final day of the season at the Winnipeg Arena. The scenario: lose the game and get the cherished "first pick."

Jets General Manager John Ferguson was salivating over that first pick. He was prepared to walk to Portland,

Oregon if he had to, to collect Dave Babych, a strong, mobile defenceman who would be the cornerstone of his franchise.

Here it was then, a strange situation: John Ferguson, one of the game's most intense competitors, a man who couldn't handle losing, pulling against his own team, HOPING to finish dead last. However, it wasn't to be. Goalie Markus Mattson performed brilliantly that day and backstopped the Jets to a 3–2 victory. The Jets would choose second. Ferguson was seething: "Can't *#&*ing win for losing! Can't *#&*ing lose for winning!"

In the end however, Ferguson did get his man with the second pick. The Montreal Canadiens, who had acquired Colorado's pick through trade, selected Doug Wickenheiser as number one overall. They chose Wickenheiser at the urging of their superstar winger, Guy Lafleur, who wanted a big centre.

Not My Bag, Man

THE JETS' FIRST COACH, Tom McVie, was a taskmaster. He always claimed he never slept, and there were some who believed him. He worked his team harder at the game-day skate than other coaches did at a practice. There was a "bag-skate" every day.

McVie was always in a hurry. In fact, he set his watch twenty minutes ahead, and if you didn't arrive on "his time," there was hell to pay. As well, club management insisted the team had to catch the first commercial flight in the morning whether they were going home or to another game that night. Thus, it was common to see a bunch of bleary-eyed Jets waiting around the airport in the early hours after playing the night before. The team would then arrive at the next city's hotel and have to wait again, because the rooms weren't ready.

McVie said the players could nap during the day, but it didn't work. Most of the first-year Jets had never played at the Montreal Forum or at Maple Leaf Gardens and were far too excited to sleep. A fact made abundantly clear when they were beaten 7–0 on their first visit to Montreal and 6–1 on their maiden journey to Toronto. Both times they had played the night before.

Fergie Launches Rocket Attack

VINCE LOMBARDI ONCE SAID, "Winning isn't everything; it's the only thing." We've all met people who seem to live by that, consciously or not. To them, a simple card game at the back of the team bus is as serious as the seventh game of the Stanley Cup Final. Bobby Clarke and Tiger Williams come to mind. So does former Blue Bomber and Maple Leaf Gerry James. Another was the late John Ferguson, whose combative spirit had no bounds. In his playing days, Ferguson had been the NHL's toughest player and a penalty king. You didn't mess with him.

In the Jets' first year, their WHA alumni invited the Montreal Canadiens Oldtimers for an exhibition game. Ferguson decided to suit up for the old Jets against his former team, and true to his nature, Fergie had to win. The referee that night was legendary Montreal Canadiens great "Rocket" Richard.

The Winnipeg Arena was packed as people anticipated a fun night with some age-old skill on display and a little humour thrown in. The Rocket thought he'd draw a chuckle by giving Ferguson a penalty. Fergie wasn't amused; in fact, he lost it. He cussed and charged at the Rocket. Richard, who was sixty years old, was having none of it and wisely hurried to the exit. The crowd at the Winnipeg Arena was embarrassed and booed their general manager. Ferguson steamed off the ice and slammed the gate so hard it reverberated through the entire building. He did not return.

The next morning, at the Jets' practice, Ferguson sat in the stands staring at his shoes, and in a very mournful, sheepish tone, said, "I've played my last hockey game."

Jimmy the Mann

IN OCTOBER OF '79 the Boston Bruins became the first "original six" team to visit the Winnipeg Jets, and there was excitement in the air. The big bad Bruins were among the elite. People came to see the Bruins more so than the Jets. The visitors had status; they were the entrée, the Jets were the leftovers. But in the end, none of that mattered as the Jets thrilled the overflow crowd with a 3–2 win. Morris Lukowich scored two goals, and a raw rookie provided the hammer. Twenty-year-old Jimmy Mann of the Jets fought tough guys Terry O'Reilly, Stan Jonathon, and Al Secord, on successive shifts, and bettered them all.

Sucker Punch

JIMMY MANN HAD A hand in one of the uglier incidents at the Winnipeg Arena. Teammate Doug Smail had just returned from a broken jaw when he took a vicious cross-check to the head from Paul Gardner of the Pittsburgh Penguins. Gardner did get a two-minute penalty but should have received five and a game misconduct. I'm sure Gardner wished he had been kicked out because he wound up paying a much stiffer price. At a stoppage in play, Jimmy Mann hopped over the boards and headed straight to where Gardner was standing, awaiting the face off. Mann didn't bother introducing himself. He sucker-punched Gardner who went down in a heap, his jaw broken in two places.

Jimmy Mann wound up with a ten-game suspension.

After the game, John Ferguson went to the dressing room and told Jimmy he was disappointed. Jimmy apologized and said he should have confronted Gardner head-on. Fergie replied that he wasn't disappointed at all by the sucker punch; he was disappointed that Gardner got up.

"If you can make it there..."

BEING AROUND JOHN FERGUSON in New York City was always a treat; he was known everywhere. In the Jets first season, Fergie took Friar and me out for a night on the town. We started at a place called "Catch a Rising Star," where various performers strutted their stuff in hopes of being discovered. It was reported that Barbara Streisand got her start there. It was a narrow, smoke-filled bar with a stage at one end. When we arrived, a drug-addled comedian with a guitar was hurling condemnation at every politician in the land. Absolutely no one was off-limits, and nothing was unsaid. I sat there stupefied, with my mouth open, while Fergie laughed knowingly. Friar pretended it was nothing new to him, but I knew better; there was nothing at all like that in Winnipeg, or his hometown Thunder Bay, or even Yorkton.

When the comedian finished his convoluted routine, the locals gave him a tremendous ovation. Then they all laughed hysterically when he fell off the stage and had to be carted away, whimpering in agony.

Next up was an actor I'd never heard of who apparently was a regular in a soap opera that was done in Hollywood. He wanted everyone to know how successful he was and how fortunate we all were to get a visit from him. That's when the booing started. By the time he got into his routine, the "Bronx cheer" drowned him out. At that point, he broke into tears and vowed he would never come back, which was when the cheering started. Then, from out of the blue, tomatoes were tossed at the stage. I was left to wonder, "Who goes to a bar with a pocketful of tomatoes?"

The next step on our night's adventure was a visit to Ferguson's friend, "Big Rich." Big Rich stood over six feet and weighed in at three hundred and fifty pounds. He owned a downtown jewelry store that had been robbed several times, but he was okay with that. "It's just the cost of doing business here; besides, I shot a couple of would-be robbers in the legs." He then took us for a drive through the city that never sleeps and pointed out the street merchants. He showed us where to go to buy flesh, drugs, stereos, whatever you happened to need at three in the morning. He pointed out several gangs, and a couple of guys hollered, "Hey Richie-man!" Friar asked Rich if he felt safe on the streets late at night. He said," I always feel safe." He then reached under the seat of his Cadillac and pulled out a sawed-off shot gun. "I got the peace maker." He then added, "I love this city; I can't imagine how anyone would want to live anywhere else. Why would you want to look at horizons when you can see all this?"

Bug Be Gone.

ONE DAY IN NEW York City, the Jet's team bus was unable to navigate a right turn due to an improperly parked Volkswagen Beetle. The bus driver was perplexed, but it wasn't a problem for John Ferguson. The Jets General Manager hollered, "Jimmy, bring a couple of the guys."

Jimmy Mann, John Ferguson, and company then stepped off the bus, picked up the car, and plopped it down on the sidewalk. Problem solved.

Where's the Hot Tar?

THE NHL DIDN'T ALWAYS televise every game, so some great visuals live only in memory. In the Jets' first season, they played in Atlanta against the Flames. The Flames had a big team and were taking liberties against the smaller Jets. Body contact and cheap shots abounded, there were fights all over the ice, and the Jets were getting pummeled. Jets Coach Tom McVie watched, seethed, then boiled over.

The benches at the OMNI in Atlanta were side-by-side. McVie began to bark at Flames coach Al MacNeil, but the jungle act continued unabated. Eventually, McVie lost it. He started by taking off his sports jacket, then loosened his tie, removed his watch, and in the ultimate act of defiance, took his teeth out. He then attempted to scale the tall glass divider between the benches. That act drew the attention of the linesmen who broke things up, while barely containing themselves at the sight of a half- dressed, growling, toothless McVie, and his quashed invasion.

Tom McVie wound up with a three-game suspension.

Set Up

AFTER THAT GAME IN Atlanta, four of us went for a drink across the street from the hotel. We were joined by former St. Louis Blues and Winnipeg Warriors scout, Dennis Ball. Dennis picked up the tab, and we were about to disperse when suddenly a complimentary drink appeared where I'd been sitting. Not wanting to appear rude, plus being a little thirsty and curious, I told everyone to go, and I would catch up in a moment. It was a rookie mistake. They were no sooner out of the door when I was presented with the same tab Dennis had just paid. When I refused to pay it, I was immediately surrounded by four of the biggest, ugliest guys I'd ever seen.

I swallowed my pride, paid the bill a second time, and left with my body parts in place.

Country Bumpkin

THE NEXT MORNING IN Atlanta, the Jets gathered at the airport to catch a flight to Washington. I got separated from the group, but that was alright; I'd just look at the big screen and see where to go to board the 8 a.m. flight. There it was, American Airlines gate A14; I'll catch the team there. However, by about 7:45, I realized I was still alone. There was nary a Winnipeg Jet in sight. Are they all lost? No. At that point I was startled to discover that there was more than one airline with an 8 a.m. direct flight from Atlanta to Washington. The flight they were on was clear on the other side of the gigantic Atlanta airport. I scurried but got there late. The team managed to hold the flight until I arrived. As I boarded the loaded plane, I could feel every eye in the place locked on me, and none was wearing a smile. Coach Tom McVie broke the silence. "Where the hell were you?" In an effort to lighten the mood, I responded loudly enough for most everyone to hear, "I got lost! The Atlanta airport is bigger than Yorkton!" A lot of people laughed; the coach was not among them.

Cowpie Anyone?

WHILE I'M ON THE topic of being worldly, I should relate more detail of my original call from Friar Nicolson in Winnipeg. He didn't actually offer me the job in that initial phone call. He, in fact, asked me to send a tape of a hockey broadcast I had done years before. I was to put it on the next Yorkton to Winnipeg flight. I said I would, and after hanging up, I thought, "What Yorkton to Winnipeg flight?" There was no such animal at that time. So, I wound up playing the tape over the phone, and apparently, he was desperate enough to hear something he liked.

The next step was to meet my prospective new bosses, Friar and CJOB Program Director John Cochrane. I drove into Winnipeg for that purpose but hit a cow en route. When I arrived for the meeting, both Friar and John were looking on as I climbed out of my not-so-shiny white Firebird with a mangled front end and cow manure plastered all over the passenger side of the vehicle. "Hi! I'm from Saskatchewan!"

Who Is Laughing Now?

ONE OF THE MOST celebrated goals ever at the Winnipeg Arena was scored by Willie Lindstrom on December 23rd, 1980. It came with less than two minutes left and gave the Jets a 5–4 win over the Colorado Rockies. 11,587 fans were delirious; it was like they'd won the Stanley Cup, but in fact, what they had done was end a thirty-game winless streak. An NHL record that stands alone to this day.

One of the oddities was that so many people sensed it would end that night. *Sports Illustrated* sent a representative, so did *The Chicago Tribune*, and other media outlets that had never shown up in Winnipeg before. All came, all saw as Lindstrom and the Jets delivered their Christmas present.

The euphoria carried over to the next game three days later when they set an attendance record, 15,766 at the Winnipeg Arena. However, they lost that Boxing Day clash 5–3 to the Minnesota North Stars.

The final tally in that season of infamy: nine wins, fifty-seven losses, and fourteen ties. Thirty-two points. It was the year they went zero for America; they didn't win a single game south of the border. They wound up with only two road wins, but it wasn't all bad, because you see, both wins were in Toronto. In their two games there, they outscored the Leafs, 10 to 2.

Christian Thing to Do

IN FEBRUARY OF THAT year, Jet Dave Christian got on a roll. He scored eleven goals in six games. The Jets lost five of them.

Twenty-four Hours
from Tulsa

WHEN YOU GO THIRTY games without a win, you're obviously in over your head. However, the Jets did have several chances to end the embarrassment much earlier. In fact, the first of the dirty thirty was at home, where they had a 4–2 lead with less than a minute to go, but the Nordiques tied it 4–4. In game four of the streak, 15,000 people at the Winnipeg Arena saw Boston's Wayne Cashman "handball" the puck into the Jets' net to tie the score 7–7. Unfortunately, there were three people who didn't see it: the lone referee and the linesmen.

In game six of the streak, the Jets had a two-goal lead in the third period only to lose in Pittsburgh. The next night they had a 4–2 lead in Washington with a minute and a half left, and it wound up 4–4. They also had third period leads of 5–2 against Calgary, and 5–3 against Boston, that both wound up 5–5. In game sixteen, the Jets lost 4–2 at home to Buffalo but did get an "A" for effort. 13,000 loyalists gave them a spontaneous standing ovation midway through the third period.

Then there was a home game against Hartford that was 5–5 after 2, and the Jets wound up losing 8–5. Jets goalie Pierre Hamel struggled that night, which wasn't surprising. He had just been called up from the farm in Tulsa, Oklahoma, and arrived in the nick of time for the game. He drove the thousand miles (1600 km).

Dubious Distinction

COVERING A TEAM THAT goes thirty games without a win is a unique experience. Those of us on the beat faced a challenge unlike anyone before or since. What to talk about? Who to talk to? The coach, Tom McVie, didn't like the media to begin with and losing made it worse. But in fairness, what was there to talk to McVie, Ferguson, or the players about? The power play?

By December, we'd exhausted the angle that things were going to get better and the Jets were only a bounce or two away from collecting a couple of wins. The losses and the occasional tie just piled up night after night. The only "out" was to tape our game-day conversations with the Jets' opponents, but that too got redundant. No matter who you talked to the answer was roughly the same, "We can't take this Jets team lightly; they've got some talent that can jump out and bite you!" It's a type of political correctness that is pushed on all teams in professional sports.

In mid-December, I spoke with Clarke Gillies, whose New York Islanders were the best team in the league, and he gave the mandatory "can't take the Jets lightly" comment but did so with a grin. After the mic was turned off, I asked what the grin was about, and he said, "If we lose this game, Coach Arbour will take every one of us to the woodshed!"

Nobody, least of all the Stanley Cup Champions, could be the first to lose. It was motivation.

Not on My Watch

IT'S USUALLY UP TO the head coach to choose his assistants. Such was not the case in the fall of '81. Tom Watt had been named the new head coach of the Winnipeg Jets. His choice of assistant was Mike Keenan, who'd had a successful run as coach of the junior Peterborough Petes. General Manager John Ferguson would have none of it. "I'm not hiring a coach who threw a game!"

It was a knock against Keenan for what had happened a few months before at the Memorial Cup tournament in Regina. Keenan's team was accused of throwing a game against the Cornwall Royals in order to avoid a meeting with the hometown Regina Pats in the final.

Ferguson insisted that Watt hire Ted Green, a Manitoban who'd had a stellar career as a defenceman with the Boston Bruins and with the WHA Jets. Watt denied the allegation against Keenan and insisted he be hired. When he realized he was getting nowhere, Watt told Ferguson, "If I can't have my man, I won't have yours!"

Bill Sutherland who had been the assistant the previous two years was retained. He and Watt hit it off well.

Peterborough and Cornwall did meet in that Memorial Cup final, and in what some considered poetic justice, the Cornwall Royals won.

The three coaches involved all went on to NHL careers. Doug Carpenter went from Cornwall to New Jersey. Mike Keenan landed in Philadelphia, and Regina Pats Coach Bryan Murray went to Washington. Murray insisted to his dying day that Keenan threw the game.

Nowhere to Go but Up

IN PROFESSIONAL SPORTS, THERE'S a system in place that rewards failure. The worse you do, the better the chance of gaining the first pick in the upcoming draft. Well, no one did worse than the '80–'81 Jets. Their thirty-two-point season had "earned" the first pick, and it was a no-brainer. Dale Hawerchuk of the Cornwall Royals was going to be a star.

It didn't take long. In his second professional game, at the tender age of eighteen, Hawerchuk scored two goals and set up two more as the Jets throttled the New York Rangers 8–3 in Winnipeg. The city and the league were abuzz. Hawerchuk would go on to score forty-five goals and collect 103 points.

But while Hawerchuk was the focal point, there were others who had super seasons as well. Veteran Jet Morris Lukowich had forty-three goals and newcomer Paul MacLean acquired from St. Louis had thirty-six. Willie Lindstrom had thirty-two goals, Dave Christian and Lucien Deblois each had twenty-five. Young Dave Babych had nineteen from the blue line. Newcomers Thomas Steen and Doug Smail weren't far behind. The goaltending too was in good hands with Eddie Staniowski and Doug Soetaert. It was a young, impressive line-up, anchored by the addition of one of the best defensemen of all time: thirty-six-year-old Serge Savard. The Jets wound up with eighty points that year and their first ever playoff berth.

One-Legged Leap Forward

THERE WERE EARLY SIGNS that success was at hand for that
'81–'82 team. In October, it took the Jets only twenty-four
hours to equal their road win total of the season before
when they managed the coveted "Alberta Double," wins
in Edmonton and Calgary. But to my mind, the real turn-
around came a month later.

Remembrance Day 1981 was a day to forget for the
Winnipeg Jets. They suffered their worst defeat ever, 15
to 2, in Minnesota. Bobby Smith had four goals and three
assists. Was this a harbinger? Were the Jets doomed to
another season of bottom-feeding?

Two nights later, that concern was put to rest. The
Jets scored a 3–2 victory in Los Angeles. The winning
goal looked like something out of a Hollywood movie.
Morris Lukowich had been hurt and was basically on one
leg when he took a breakaway pass from Thomas Steen,
hobbled in, and scored the winner with six seconds left.
There was something in that goal, and at that moment,
that indicated all was well.

Something Good from Something Bad

IMMEDIATELY AFTER THE 15–2 debacle in Minnesota, I was surprised to see John Ferguson, Tom Watt, and Bill Sutherland in the hotel bar. I approached with caution, unsure how they would react to company. Amazingly, they were in good spirits. They had chosen to laugh it off. They did, however, arrange to get the hell out of Minnesota a day earlier than planned. As well, late that night Ferguson placed another in a series of calls to defenceman Serge Savard, pleading with the former Montreal Canadien great to unretire. "Serge, we just lost 15 to *#&*ing 2!" The degree of desperation in his old buddy's voice led to a change of heart, and shortly after, Serge Savard and family brought their "savoir faire" to Winnipeg.

Get offa' My Cloud Kid

AS A RESULT OF their unprecedented improvement (forty-eight points) from year two to year three, Tom Watt was named "Coach of the Year," and Dale Hawerchuk was "Rookie of the Year."

Early the following season, the Jets were beaten soundly at home by the Minnesota North Stars, who were the defending Western champions. After the game, Hawerchuk was bitter and he complained to the media. "How are we going to beat the league finalists playing four lines when they're going with three? We can't compete that way!"

The following day at practice, Hawerchuk was greeted by a very subtle message. The Jack Adams "Coach of the Year" trophy was sitting proudly in Hawerchuk's stall. Watt's unspoken message was loud and clear.

That wasn't the only lesson handed to the young phenom by his coach. Another time Dale was complaining about his shifts being too short. Watt asked the eighteen-year-old how long they should be? Dale replied, "Two minutes." The coach grabbed his stopwatch and made a deal with his prize rookie. "If you can go all out for one full minute, I'll give you three-minute shifts if you want!" A half-minute later, a huffing and puffing Hawerchuk fully understood why the ideal NHL shift is under forty seconds.

Feisty and Reverent
Don't Mix

IN MORRIS LUKOWICH, WHAT you saw is what you got. He was straightforward and dedicated to his craft. In the Jets' nine-win season ('80–'81) he scored thirty-three goals.

I recall taping an interview with Lukowich and being amazed at how forthright he was. The interview was to run in the intermission of that night's game. Mid-afternoon, Lukowich phoned and asked, "Curt, can we do that interview over again? I said things I shouldn't have." I replied, "No problem, we'll do it tonight at the rink." A half-hour later, my phone rang again, and it was Lukowich. "I wouldn't have said all those things if they weren't true so, go ahead and run the interview." It was vintage Lukowich; he could not have been a politician.

Normally Lukowich gave no quarter, but there was an exception. He was face to face with Wayne Gretzky when the "Great One" kneed him in the midsection. To the shock of everyone, Lukowich did not retaliate. He just stood there, dumbfounded. I asked him about it. His reply, "I didn't sleep last night. I'm totally embarrassed. I just looked at him and thought, 'What do I do? He's Wayne Gretzky!'" Lukowich then added, "If he ever does anything like that again, I'll cold-cock him." Such was the incredible reverence that a young Gretzky commanded around the league. It wasn't all "fear of Semenko."

Dave "Sammy" Semenko was among the most feared people to ever play the game. If you touched Gretzky, Semenko would exact a price. In the heat of action, Gretzky was often heard to say, "Sammy'll get you."

Willie Wows Philly

THERE WAS SOMETHING FOREBODING about the Spectrum in Philadelphia. Although the Broad Street Bullies has disbanded several years earlier, their ghosts remained. The building itself was small. The seats were crimson like a deep shade of blood. The fans were near the ice, and they were ornery. You half expected them to appear in togas with their thumbs down. It took some manhood to stand out at the Spectrum.

In March of '82, the Jets went to the Spectrum and beat the Flyers 7–6. Willie Lindstrom scored five goals and set up another. The inappropriate term "Chicken-Swede" died that night.

The Flyers pulled their goaltender in the last minute, but Coach Tom Watt chose not to put Lindstrom on the ice. He felt the distraction of looking for goal six could cost his team a victory.

Prairie People Don't Forget

IN THE '80S, THE NHL preseason was a marathon. Teams played as many as ten games, and it wasn't uncommon to play three in three nights in three different cities. Early in the preseason, there'd be sixty players to draw from on any given night. The rule of thumb was to play the extras on the road and play the name players and top prospects at home.

That was all well and good until you met at a neutral venue. In the early '80s, the Jets were the designated home team for a September game in Regina. The spanking new Regina Agridome was filled to capacity. Everyone was there to see celebrated hockey players strut their stuff in the flesh. Except on this night, most of the big names were absent. The P.A. announcer began to list the Jet scratches and the boos began: "Dale Hawerchuk...Paul MacLean... Thomas Steen...Dave Babych" and the list went on. The Jets as a group became persona non grata in Regina. The only "names" the Jets dressed were Saskatchewan-born Morris Lukowich and Eddie Staniowski. Staniowski played brilliantly in gaining a shutout, but it did nothing to appease the crowd. Six thousand people felt cheated, and John Ferguson was embarrassed. The Jets' general manager hadn't been made aware that the game was a hot ticket. Long before the game was over, Ferguson vowed to return to Regina the following year and bring the "A" team.

Ferguson lived up to his promise, but the damage was done. Virtually nobody showed up to watch.

All In, All the Time

I WENT TO SEE John Ferguson in the first intermission one night in Calgary. What I saw was a man whose white shirt was drenched in perspiration, and his face was crimson. He was livid over what he'd seen in that first period and unleashed a profanity-laced diatribe. The thing was, it was September. It was a preseason game. No more than ten of the players in Jets uniforms that night would be with the club a month later when the season began. In John Ferguson's world, there were no exhibition games.

Terrific Tandem

ONE OF THE GREAT memories of watching the Jets play 1400 times was the penalty killing pairing of Ron Wilson and Doug Smail. They were buzz saws; there was no holding back. They would pursue the puck at either end of the ice, and if they got caught, each had the speed to recover. They created chaos, forced turnovers, and were a constant offensive threat. Doug Smail scored a club record twenty-five shorthanded goals for the Jets.

Smail was the last of the original NHL Jets to wear number nine; a number retired in the name of Bobby Hull.

Hull's jersey retirement ceremony was one of the classiest ever at the Winnipeg Arena. The Golden Jet skated a lap in full uniform, as Gordie Howe, Ab McDonald, and many of Hull's contemporaries looked on. The crowd went wild. The ceremony was supposed to conclude with Smail removing jersey number nine and presenting it to Hull. However, that didn't happen, because Smail had been left in a Detroit hospital recovering from "friendly fire." A wayward Freddy Olausson slapshot had broken his face.

But You're Done, Tom!

TOM WATT WAS "COACH of the Year" for the '81–'82 season. His club had achieved an unprecedented forty-eight-point improvement over the year before. Jets fans, management, and owners were pumped; this team was on the road to glory. They had five players with twenty-five goals or more led by teenage phenom Dale Hawerchuk, who'd won the Calder trophy.

But as was their lot, the Jets struggled the following year. They finished under five hundred and barely got into the playoffs, where they were eliminated in straight games by the Edmonton Oilers. Thus, the natives became restless. Ticket sales going into Watt's third season were tough. The team had to get out of the gate quickly. However, after fourteen games, they had only four wins. Things were butt ugly.

With this background, I went to the Winnipeg Arena on the morning of November 6th, 1983. There I had a chance encounter with Jets President Barry Shenkarow who told me that coach Tom Watt would be fired the next morning. I asked, "What happens if the Jets win tonight against the Edmonton Oilers?" Shenkarow replied, "It won't matter. He's done."

Immediately after that conversation, I went to the Jets' dressing room to do my daily interview with the head coach. We discussed the upcoming game, the opponent, his line-up. When that was done, Tom began telling me about the renovations he had in mind for his office and the dressing room. It was strange. The whole time he was talking about the future, Shenkarow's statement was echoing in my head. "He's done."

Then came the game, and what a game it was. Early in the second period Robert Picard nearly brought the house down with a shorthanded goal that made the score 3–0 Jets. I was wearing a curious smile but couldn't say why. How would they justify firing the coach at this rate? Then Gretzky happened. Wayne Gretzky had what his coach Glen Sather said was his finest hour to that point in his career. In the last half of the game, Gretzky scored four goals and assisted three more. The Oilers beat the Jets 8 to 5.

The next morning General Manager John Ferguson announced that Watt was fired and claimed that blowing the three-goal lead had sealed his fate. Ferguson said losing that way is something that should never happen in the NHL.

Ferguson took over as interim coach for the next six games, finishing two and four. In two of the four losses, the Jets blew three goal leads.

Mon Dieu!

IN THE EARLY '80s, the Winnipeg Jets chartered a bus to go from Montreal to Quebec City for a game that night with the Nordiques. To no one's surprise, it was snowing; it seemed it always snowed on that trip. This time though, it was a little heavier than usual and visibility was restricted. The players, coaches, and the rest of us were unconcerned. Everybody did their own thing: some played cards, others slept, some read, and others listened to their Walkmans.

Then suddenly everything changed. Ahead on the divided highway was a semi-trailer that had jackknifed and was blocking both lanes. The bus driver touched the brake to no avail. The bus began to fishtail; we were on a bed of black ice! There was no way to avoid a collision with the semi!

That's when we witnessed a driving exhibition for the ages. The driver wheeled the skidding bus into the ditch, separating the eastbound and westbound lanes. The bus blasted through snow that appeared to be above the wheel wells and came up on the other side of the highway. It was brilliant except for one thing: we were now headed the wrong way on a one-way!

We continued that way for a while; the bus was deathly quiet. Oncoming traffic stayed in their righthand lane. Until, in the distance through the driving snow, we could make out a semi in "our" lane passing another semi. He was coming right at us! A head on collision was imminent. Then again, our French- speaking driver wheeled to the right, ploughed through the snowbanks separating the lanes and emerged on the proper side of the highway. The cheering on that bus rivaled anything you've ever heard in a "white-out." The bus driver was everybody's hero!

We all shook the driver's hand, and the team greased his palm, but I don't know his name, and I wish I did. I'd shout it from the rooftops. The man saved thirty young lives; he should be given a public salute in Winnipeg. In the meantime, all I can offer is, "Merci monsieur" (whoever or wherever you are.)

We had to ride the same bus back to Montreal after the game, so for that reason, we didn't mention the highway scare "on air." (We didn't want wives and families fretting.) Come to think of it, the newspaper guys (Pat Doyle and Reyn Davis) must have kept mum as well because I don't recall anyone ever asking me about it.

A Rock and a Hard Place

I DON'T KNOW IF anybody has ever pulled a goalie in playoff overtime, but the Jets nearly did in '84. Game two of their playoff series in Edmonton was tied 4–4 and going to extra time. Marc Behrend was in goal for the Jets and had played well. The thing was, Behrend had played most of the season with the U.S. Olympic team, and by the time he arrived in Winnipeg, he wasn't in NHL shape. Could he hold up for overtime? Coaches Barry Long, Rick Bowness, and Bill Sutherland could see Behrend was near exhaustion, so what do you do? If you bring a goalie in cold and he's beaten, you look like a fool. They left him in, and you guessed it: he gave up a "softie" to Randy Gregg twenty-one seconds into overtime.

What a Party!

IN THE EARLY MORNING hours of April 15, 1985, the Winnipeg airport was a madhouse. The place was filled with ecstatic fans who had waited all night to greet their conquering heroes. The Jets had beaten the Flames 5–3 in Calgary to claim their first ever playoff series win. The party went all night and well into the next day; Mardi Gras would have paled! What made it all the more impressive is that the Jets delivered the crowning blow without the aid of their star. Dale Hawerchuk had suffered cracked ribs in the previous game and was out for the duration of the playoffs.

It was the highlight of the Jets' most magical season. They had entered the playoffs as the hottest team in the league, unbeaten in thirteen games. They were an offensive juggernaut boasting six, thirty-goal scorers and two others with over twenty. They were pure entertainment.

(*Dale Hawerchuk scored fifty-three goals, Paul MacLean scored forty-one, Brian Mullen and Laurie Boschman each had thirty-two, Doug Smail scored thirty-one, and Thomas Steen, thirty.*)

Sky's the Limit

IN MID-MARCH OF THAT year, the Jets had just begun their run. They'd gone to Montreal and won 4–1. They were getting better every night. I was beginning to believe they were on the cusp of something special. To find out if it was real, I went to a man for whom I had immeasurable respect, assistant coach Bill Sutherland and asked, "How far can they go?" Without hesitation, he said, "This team can go all the way." The next night they went to Quebec City and beat the Nordiques, and two nights later scored a 5–3 victory over the Buffalo Sabres. I didn't need any more affirmation.

They didn't achieve the pinnacle, of course, their season ending as it so often did at the hands of the vaunted Edmonton Oilers, but it was a great ride.

Victims of Geography

IN THAT '84–'85 SEASON, the top three teams in the west all played in the same (Smythe) division, #1 Edmonton, #2 Winnipeg, and #3 Calgary, and it wasn't even close. The third-place Flames were eight points better than the St. Louis Blues, who finished atop the other western (Norris) division.

However, it didn't matter. By the format of the day, each division had to declare its own winner, so Smythe met Smythe in the first two rounds. That guaranteed that one of the top three western teams would not make it beyond round one, and it further guaranteed that only one of the top three teams could possibly make it to the Western final. It was a bad system, particularly for the Jets. Most times the Oilers advanced, sometimes the Flames did, but the Jets never got beyond round two.

The Sutherland Code

JOHN FERGUSON WAS AN unabashed "hands-on" general manager. He was never hesitant about going to the dressing room between periods to let his coaches know what they were doing wrong. His shouting matches with coach Tom Watt were legendary; you could hear them a mile away. Fergie was adamant, but Watt may have been the most stubborn man on the planet.

Sometime after Watt's departure, Barry Long became the head coach. Long too, was often the recipient of his boss' unsolicited advice. On the "Coach's Show" before every game, I was subtly informed of the reason behind any personnel change. I'd ask Long a question, and if the answer came out directly, then it was his decision, but if he winked, I knew his hand had been forced. It was radio, so it was totally harmless, but I always appreciated the trust and the knowledge.

Long's assistants were Bill Sutherland and Rick Bowness. Sutherland was the "eye in the sky" and would transmit suggestions to Bowness behind the bench. The problem was, Ferguson often sat right beside Sutherland in the press box and, as you may have guessed, had no shortage of advice to be passed along. It led to confusion. Mixed signals were being sent to the bench, so the coaches devised a strategy. If Sutherland prefaced his comment to Bowness by saying "Rick," that meant it was coming from Ferguson; if he used the nickname "Bones," it was coming from Sutherland.

The hardest part for Sutherland was keeping a straight face when Ferguson would cry out, "It's like they're not hearing a #@#ing word I say!"

Misfire

IN OCTOBER OF '85, the Jets took a 3–0 first period lead over the Flames in Calgary but lost 8 to 3. Along the way, Jet goaltender Bryan Hayward got a game misconduct for an altercation with Flames tough guy Tim Hunter. It was the ultimate mismatch. The Jets cleared their bench, and others not noted for their pugilistic prowess also got tossed, defensemen Tim Watters and Dave Ellet. As well, Jets assistant coach Rick Bowness was evicted for accidentally punching linesman Randy Mitton. Bowness was standing on the Jets bench when he delivered a haymaker intended for Tim Hunter but missed and nailed Mitton.

Bowness was suspended for three games.

The Calgary Herald came out with a great front-page picture of that errant punch, and it fetched a good price at a charity auction in Winnipeg. The buyer was Coach Bowness.

Heady Stuff

A MID-'80S MEETING BETWEEN the Winnipeg Jets and the Edmonton Oilers usually meant great entertainment with plenty of speed and scoring chances. However, a December '85 meeting at the Winnipeg Arena took on a decidedly different twist.

Once again, the Jets took a 3–0 lead over the Oilers, only to lose 6 to 3. As well that night, the Jets lost much of their defense. Jim Kyte hurt his fist, slamming the head of Marty McSorley, and couldn't finish the game. Defenceman Bobby Dollas earned a game misconduct. Tim Watters drew a ten-minute misconduct, while the other three blue liners, Mario Marois, Dave Ellet, and Wade Campbell, spent much of the night serving minor penalties. Jet centre Thomas Steen played most of the game as a defenceman.

Oiler Glen Anderson and Jet Dave Silk got into a stick-swinging duel that ended when Anderson struck Silk in the head. Anderson got a rare ten-minute major. Wayne Gretzky protested the call and got the biggest ovation of the night when he was handed a ten-minute misconduct.

A day or two later, Anderson was assessed an eight-game suspension while Silk got six.

Fergie's Ice Bucket

IN THE EARLY DAYS of the Winnipeg Jets, the game entertainment wasn't restricted to what took place on the ice. The fans too were a story, the white outs became legendary, there was an intimacy there that you wouldn't expect to find in a gathering of fifteen thousand plus. As well, many of the fans had a pretty good view of the press box. They would notice some of the names of the game located there, it might have been Harold Ballard and King Clancy, maybe Gordie Howe or Bobby Orr.

People also noticed when changes were made. So, when suddenly the Jets general manager's box became enclosed in shaded glass, people were disappointed and wondered why? One of their favourite pastimes had been watching the reaction of John Ferguson when things didn't go right; he was spontaneous combustion. It could be brought on by a goal against, a giveaway, an errant pass, or particularly by a bad call. Fergie hated referees. In his world, a penalty should only be called if you carried a gun.

So why was he encased in glass? Well, according to word on the street, it was bulletproofing. Fergie had been getting death threats and it was done for his protection. It was a story the Jets chose not to rebuke, and while there was some truth to it (threats), it wasn't the real story. The fact is, it was done to shield visiting coaches and players. You see, Ferguson's location was directly above the visiting player's bench. I can still see the look on the face of Buffalo Sabres coach Scotty Bowman when he stared skyward after being hit on the head by the remnants of Fergie's ice bucket.

Sign "4" the Times

MANY SPORTS TEAMS WON'T allow people to display "signs" during events. The official reasoning is that they may be in poor taste or may obstruct the view of other fans. Fair enough, but there is often a more self-serving purpose for sign banishment. It is to restrict freedom of expression during troubled times for the home team, a time when the paying public is antsy and looking for heads to roll.

1985–'86 was to be the "season of the Jets," a time for fans to rejoice and give it back to their arrogant Alberta neighbours. The Edmonton Oilers, in large part and the Calgary Flames to a lesser degree, had used the Jets as a stepping-stone on the road to playoff glory. Jets fans were bitter, resentful, jealous. Things had to change, and this would be the year. This year justice would be served, and revenge would be sweet.

Well, once again, things didn't go as planned. The precious Jets were under achieving. In looking for someone to blame, the fans fixed their cannons squarely on General Manager John Ferguson. The cry of "Fire Fergie" was heard on the airwaves and seen on crudely made signs at the Winnipeg Arena.

So, prior to each game, the beleaguered general manager would call over his personal assistant David "Skully" Mann. Ferguson would point to different signs around the arena and tell his faithful associate to get rid of them. Skully cherished the responsibility and did his job well. Except one night. There was a sign that had Fergie's name on it but, was it negative? No one could figure it out. The sign stayed up all night. It wasn't until very late that somebody deduced the meaning, and it was classic.

At the beginning of that season, the number "4" figured prominently on Jets jerseys, but that had changed dramatically.

At the beginning, Wade Campbell wore number 4 for the Jets, but he was traded to Boston. Number 14 Anssi Melametsa went back to Finland. Number 24 Ron Wilson had been demoted to Springfield. Number 34 Dave Silk had been dealt to the Rangers, and number 44 Dave Babych was traded to Hartford.

The sign read simply, "Give Fergie number 54."

Fergie's Folly

IN LIGHT OF ALL the negativity, Ferguson's legendary lack of patience was being severely tested. Eruptions from his press box perch at the Winnipeg Arena were commonplace. There would be a resounding "bang" as one of his fabled fists collided with the wall beside him. The impact was such that the whole press box would shake. That would be followed by a muffled series of expletives, muffled only because the room was entirely enclosed. Well, it didn't take long to realize that each eruption was immediately preceded by something Dave Babych did or didn't do. He may have coughed up the puck, or failed to shoot, or maybe didn't hit somebody. At that point, it was obvious that Babych's days as a Jet were numbered. We asked the Jets general manager if his big defenceman was on the trade block. He replied, "Of course not. Where would you get a silly idea like that?" John never did figure out how we often knew who he would trade before the deal was done.

After a home game with the St. Louis Blues, the shoe fell. The announcement was immediate. Babych was going to the Hartford Whalers in exchange for Ray Neufeld. A trade immediately greeted by skepticism by everyone who followed hockey closely and treated with disdain by Winnipeg hockey fans. Ray Neufeld? He was a Manitoban; they knew that. He scored a few goals; they knew that. But basically, he was a "plugger," an effective winger. Babych, on the other hand, was a "horse" who could manage the blue line effectively for thirty minutes a night.

Three days later, the Jets played in Hartford against Babych and the Whalers. The result, an 8–1 Whaler win. In the process, it became apparent who had won the trade, and it wasn't Ferguson.

One thing you never saw was John Ferguson alone in a bar. In fact, after a loss, you generally didn't see him at all until the next day. But that night in Hartford was different. There he was, well after midnight, bellied up to the hotel bar alone, a scotch in hand and a "hangdog" look on his face. He caught sight of radio host Mike O'Hearn and me and called us in. I've never seen a man so depressed. He'd screwed up, and he knew it. He chastised himself repeatedly. He then insisted we come up to his seventh-floor room for a nightcap. We did. He phoned his old buddy and former coach Tom McVie and lamented the trade. Afterward McVie asked to speak with me. His words: "Stay with Fergie, I think he might jump."

Oh, What a Night It Was, It Really Was!

ON THE 8TH OF November 1986, Winnipeg was hit by a crippling blizzard, thirty-five centimeters of fresh snow. If you didn't have a 4x4 vehicle or skis, you were immobilized. You weren't going anywhere for three days unless, of course, the Jets were playing. Thousands who were unable to make it to work did manage to file into the Winnipeg Arena; some arrived wearing snowshoes.

It wasn't even assured there would be a game that night. The airport had been closed until late in the afternoon and the New Jersey Devils arrived in the nick of time. The Devils bus only got to about a block away from the arena; the players filed out, grabbed take-out burgers, and each threw an equipment bag over his shoulder and marched down Maroons Road to the Arena. It was vintage "Canadiana."

The crowd was announced as 10,722, and while it was well short of that "official" figure, it was an incredible show of support. The hardy group didn't go through wind and snow to sit on their hands either. They were in party mode, and the Jets responded with an 8–1 victory.

Who's on First?

IN A MID-'80S PLAYOFF series, the Winnipeg Jets ran into a goaltending dilemma. The goaltending was so bad; it led to a trivia question that's never been asked. What NHL team used the most goaltenders in the shortest series? Answer: the 1986 Winnipeg Jets.

Late that season, General Manager John Ferguson had fired Barry Long and taken over the coaching reins himself. His first move was to go with the veteran Dan Bouchard as his main man between the pipes. Long had leaned toward Brian Hayward.

When they got to the playoffs, the Jets went to Calgary, and Ferguson started Bouchard. However, the veteran had a bad night and was pulled after the second period. Brian Hayward went in and didn't surrender a goal, but it didn't matter; the Flames cruised to a 5–1 win.

In game two, Bouchard didn't even dress. Hayward started and he too was bad. Hayward was lifted in the third period and replaced by Marc Behrend, who didn't give up a goal, but again it didn't matter; the Flames won 6–4.

The best of five series shifted to Winnipeg for game three. On that night, neither Bouchard nor Hayward dressed, and Behrend was the backup. The goalie was Daniel Berthiaume, straight up from the Quebec Junior league. The kid played a stellar game but fell just short as Lanny Macdonald scored in overtime to give the Flames the series sweep.

The Jets used four goalies in a three-game playoff series.

It's Alright to Be White

IN THE SPRING OF '87, when told of the "White Out" promotion the Winnipeg Jets were launching for the playoffs, I was skeptical. The idea was appealing but the follow-through could be appalling, or so I thought. I was wrong, again, and glad of it. The "White Out" was a resounding success everywhere but on the ice; it was incredible! The whole arena was bathed in "motion" white. It swayed, it rocked, and it was loud. You could not hear the person beside you because his voice was outnumbered 15,000 to 1.

And there's something about dressing up that "outs" a lot of people; it seemed everyone was an extrovert. Some were more colourful than others. There was a group of nine or ten lawyers who all wore face masks of famous people, and they were ultra-demonstrative. There was Winston Churchill, Ronald Reagan, Margaret Thatcher, Pierre Trudeau, and there may have been an Abraham Lincoln sighting. They mocked the visiting players. There was a lady in a wedding dress with a giant "Marry Me Khabby" sign directed at Jet goalie Nikolai Khabibulin. Sir Galahad was spotted in the parking lot astride a big white horse.

White Out night was party night, not just at the rink but at the bars and restaurants as well. Make that IS party night; the new regime has maintained the tradition. Good on 'em.

Tumultuous Times

IN THE SUMMER OF 1988, the Winnipeg Jets traded away their perennial forty-goal man, Paul MacLean; it was the start of something ugly. Over the course of the following season, there were firings, there was discontent, and there was even indifference. John Ferguson was fired as general manager after only eight games and was replaced by Mike Smith. In February, Dan Maloney was fired as coach and replaced by Rick Bowness.

Between times the Jets divested themselves of Mario Marois, Alain Chevrier, Dave Hunter, and Ray Neufeld. In January, Captain Dale Hawerchuk complained that the Jets kept trading people away and getting nothing in return. He said they were dumping contracts, and he wanted out if things didn't change.

The Jets two goalies, dubbed "Pokey and the Bandit," weren't getting along with each other and neither was playing well. Meanwhile, goalie Alain Chevrier, who'd been deemed expendable, was the toast of the Chicago Black Hawks.

That Jet team was a mess.

Polar Opposites

THERE WERE NEVER TWO more different people than the first and second general managers of the NHL Jets. The first, John Ferguson, was bombastic and commanding. The second, Mike Smith, was subdued and contemplative. John Ferguson wore tailored suits with the perfect tie. Mike Smith wore suits off the rack, and the tie askew. John Ferguson lived in the exclusive Tuxedo area of Winnipeg. His license plate read, "JETS 1." Mike Smith rented a condo in the Exchange District.

On a scouting trip, John Ferguson would rent a Cadillac and hire a porter. Mike Smith would rent a Chevy and was known to carry a backpack. Ferguson would stay in the executive suite at the Ritz. Smith would stay at Motel 6. Ferguson travelled with an entourage that would accommodate his every wish and laugh heartily at every joke. When Smith was fired by the Jets, he took a trip overseas, alone.

Ferguson read the *Horse Racing Digest*. Smith read *The Bolshevik Revolution*.

Ferguson liked North American hockey players in his own image, tough as nails. Smith had a penchant for free-skating Russians. Ferguson liked old-school dictatorial coaches like Tom McVie. Smith liked the cerebral approach and imported Alpo Suhonen. Ferguson was a graduate of junior hockey. Smith graduated with a doctorate in Sociology. Ferguson coddled many of his players. Smith kept them all at arm's length.

Hammerin' Hank

HOCKEY'S "BLACK ACES" ARE the guys who practice long hours every day but don't get to play. Its drudgery and they hate it, at least most do. Hannu Jarvenpaa was the exception. He sat through ten consecutive games in 1988 and wouldn't get back into the lineup until someone was hurt. Well, one night in Washington, Doug Smail was caught by the skate of Rod Langway and got a twenty-two-stitch cut to the back of his leg. When Jarvenpaa was told he'd replace Smail the next night in Philadelphia, he replied, "Oh no, Dougie can play!" Whoops. Coach Dan Maloney was livid; he wanted Jarvenpaa on the next plane back to Finland. Fortunately for Jarvenpaa, the new general manager, Mike Smith, opted to give him another chance. Jarvenpaa responded in Philadelphia by hitting every Flyer in sight and earning the short-lived moniker "Hammerin' Hank."

Be-leaf It

IN MARCH OF 1989, Jet Dale Hawerchuk had a six-point game against the Toronto Maple Leafs. It was the third six-point night of his career, and every one of them came at Maple Leaf Gardens in Toronto with his family looking on.

Another oddity that year, in a 9–7 loss to the Jets, Toronto defenceman Borje Salming finished plus six.

Standing amidst greatness.

Blue Bomber Willard Reaves, and the man who left us much too soon, Dale Hawerchuk.

Don't Fix What's Not Broken

COACHES ARE USUALLY PREDICTABLE; they'll err on the side of caution. They'd much rather talk about defense than offense. There are always some however, who break from the doctrine. Jet coach Barry Long admitted to enjoying a 6–5 game more than a 2–1. I remember Calgary Flames coach Al MacNeil telling me that he didn't care if Kent Nilsson ever saw his own side of centre ice as long as he got a hundred points. Then there was Bob Murdoch. Every time the Jets would lose a game he would say, "Well, we learned something today." He never did say what it was they learned.

In the playoffs of 1990, Murdoch convinced many of us that coaching logic and common sense can be at odds. It was the year of the Dave Ellet double-overtime goal. The Jets had earned a 3–2 series lead over Edmonton and were looking to wrap it up at home. Prior to game six, Murdoch called a power play meeting. Dave Ellet suggested the coach wait a minute because Dale Hawerchuk wasn't in the room. The coach replied, "No, Dale's not on the power play tonight." The Jets then went out and fell behind 3–0 in the first period in part because the power play went 0 for 4. After the first period, Hawerchuk was reinserted on the power play, and the Jets did come back to tie it, but ultimately lost the game 4–3. Hawerchuk said afterward that Coach Murdoch was always trying to "reinvent the wheel."

Huh?

FORWARD TO GAME SEVEN of that series, and Murdoch had everyone scratching their heads again. It concerned his goaltending choice. But first, a little background. All season long Murdoch had alternated goaltenders. It was Bob Essensa and Daniel Berthiaume early on, then after a trade, Essensa alternated with Stephane Beauregard. The Jets had a ho-hum regular season, thirty-seven wins and thirty-two losses. The goaltending numbers though told a different story; Essensa was eighteen and nine, Beauregard was seven and eight. It seemed a clear case to make "Goalie Bob" the playoff netminder.

He was in game one, and the Jets won it. Beauregard played game two and the Oilers won in overtime. Essensa came back for game three and the Jets won 2–1. At that point, Murdoch broke his rotation and started Essensa a second straight time. However, Essensa suffered a minor injury part way through, and Beauregard mopped up in that celebrated double-overtime win. Beauregard then played game five, and the Oilers prevailed 4–3. Essensa was back for game six in Winnipeg and suffered his only playoff defeat 4–3.

So going into game seven, Essensa was two and one in the series and twenty and ten on the year. Beauregard was one and two in the series and eight and ten on the year. Murdoch's goaltending choice: Beauregard. It was one of the strangest coaching decisions ever, and what's more, Jets assistant coaches Clare Drake and Alpo Suhonen were in complete accord with Murdoch. I know the players didn't agree, nor did the fans or the media. The Oilers won the game 4–1, the series 4–3, and ultimately won the Stanley Cup.

New Kids in Town

IN THE EARLY '90s, the Winnipeg Jets scouting staff was on a roll. They made a series of outstanding draft picks and waited patiently until after the 1992 Olympics to bring them all together. On opening night of the 92–93 season, they dressed seven rookies. Two of them didn't make it long-term: Sergei Bautin and Winnipegger Russ Romaniuk. A third player will be discussed later.

The other four became known as the "Young Guns." They included Evgeny Davydov, a free-spirited Russian who scored twenty-eight goals that year. He was fun to watch but totally off the wall. He would gain control of the puck and circle incessantly for no particular reason. How much the coaching staff trusted him became apparent when they sat him out of the final two playoff games.

The other three rookies were incredible; they formed the Jets "Olympic Line." At centre, the red-headed Russian, Alexei Zhamnov; he was gifted but not as motivated as his wingers. On the left side was rugged Keith Tkachuk, a Bostonian with attitude, the prototypical power forward. And on the right was a speedy sniper from Finland, Teemu Selanne.

The Jets won that opening game 4–1 over Detroit. Tkachuk had a goal and an assist. Selanne had two assists, and Zhamnov had one. It was the start of something special.

Blew That One

IN THE FALL OF 1990, the Jets brought a baby-faced nineteen-year-old to training camp who immediately impressed everybody. He could skate like the wind and had a great attitude. I never saw anybody more excited to get an NHL tryout. When the Jets sent him back to junior in Ottawa, he thanked everyone for the chance and vowed to return.

He was then named to Canada's National Junior team and was "player of the game" in the gold medal final victory over Russia.

He returned to Winnipeg as one of the seven opening night rookies in '92. It appeared he would be a big part of the Jets future, but not so. In a move that would forever haunt the Jets, they sold the player to the Detroit Red Wings for one dollar.

Kris Draper collected four Stanley Cup rings with the Red Wings.

Another That Got Away

I NEVER UNDERSTOOD WHY the NHL scouted American colleges so extensively while virtually ignoring Canadian University hockey. The Winnipeg Jets, among others, paid a price for that.

In the mid-'80s, the acknowledged best player in Canadian College hockey was Mike Ridley. Ridley was a Winnipegger who played for the University of Manitoba. He was never drafted. Ridley's dream was to play for the Winnipeg Jets. He asked for a training camp invite in 1986 but was refused. Instead, he went to the camp of the New York Rangers. He made the all-rookie team that year and had an illustrious twelve-year NHL career over which he collected 752 points.

Lost in the Wash

THROUGH THE FIRST THIRTY-FIVE games of their rookie seasons, Teemu Selanne and Keith Tkachuk had thirty-nine goals between them, but it wasn't enough; the Jets were losing. They had only thirteen wins against nineteen losses (and three ties.) Something needed to be done and was. Three days after Christmas, General Manager Mike Smith dealt talent for toughness. Eddy Olczyk was sent to the New York Rangers for Kris King and Tie Domi. Domi brought the house down by scoring the first time he touched the puck, and the Jets beat the Boston Bruins 5–4. Domi and King provided boldness to the entire team. The Jets won twenty-seven and lost eighteen the rest of the way and were rewarded with a playoff berth.

Goal Fifty-four, Where Are You?

BY MID-FEBRUARY OF 1993 there was no question that Teemu Selanne was going to become the highest scoring rookie in the history of the National Hockey league. The only questions were when would it happen, and where? Everybody, including Selanne wanted it to happen in Winnipeg. However, by February 27th, it was impossible. Selanne had forty-seven goals, the record of Mike Bossy was fifty-three. The Jets had only two games at home before embarking on a five-game road trip. The best people could hope for was that the "Finnish Flash" would score three and achieve the fifty mark in the friendly confines of the Winnipeg Arena.

On February 28th, the Minnesota North Stars were in town. The Jets beat the Stars 7–6. Selanne scored goals number forty-eight, forty-nine, fifty, and fifty-one. The Winnipeg Arena was bedlam.

The crowd count the night Selanne scored four was only 11,700. Two nights later, when the Quebec Nordiques came to town, it was 14,400. Prior to the game, I wandered through the lobby and asked people what they were expecting that night? Without exception, every person said they came to see Teemu's hat trick. None had any doubt that the rookie would score three times and pass Mike Bossy. They were there to witness history.

The celebrating began early. Fifteen seconds into the game, a Selanne breakaway made it 1–0; it was goal number fifty-two. The Nordiques then scored three in a row. The Jets closed it to 3–2 when Selanne struck again, this time on a wraparound; his fifty-third goal tied Mike Bossy. By the third period it was 3–3, then came the moment Jet fans will never forget. Tie Domi flipped the puck out of the Jets end; it landed in Nordiques territory. There was a race for the puck that Hollywood would have done in slow motion. Would Selanne get to it or goalie Stephane Fiset? Selanne did, barely, and flipped it over the sliding netminder into the gaping net. History!

I'm sometimes asked what was the most impressive thing I saw in 2400 NHL games? Well, given the circumstance, it was those seven goals in two games. Had Selanne been a Toronto Maple Leaf we'd still be seeing it replayed. Had he been a New York Ranger we'd still be reading about it.

There was a wild celebration after the goal that culminated in an on- ice ceremony where Selanne was presented with a Silver Stick by Jet President Barry Shenkarow. When the action resumed everyone but the Nordiques had lost their focus. Quebec scored four goals in less than four minutes and beat the Jets 7–4.

Too Much "Mr. Nice Guy"

SEVEN GOALS IN TWO games wasn't the end of it for the "Finnish Flash." Two days later in Edmonton, he scored two and assisted two in a 5–4 win. Nine goals in three games, and wouldn't you know the next stop was Toronto on a Saturday night. The media crush at the morning skate was immense, and as always Selanne accommodated every interviewer and every autograph seeker. As a result, the rookie missed the team meal and didn't get back to the hotel until three o'clock. Coach John Paddock was justifiably incensed. That night Selanne played well for three shifts in the first period, then did nothing. The streak ended, and presumably a lesson was learned.

I believe that was the night that Selanne and Tkachuk were benched in the third period. At one stage Teemu asked Keith, "Why aren't we playing?" To which, the ever straight forward Tkachuk replied, "Because we're playing the shits."

Who Is This Lady Byng?

THERE WAS ALWAYS A particular seating order on the team bus. The general manager and coaches sat in the first couple of rows, the writers and broadcasters in the next couple with the rookies right behind, and the veterans to the back. The more the seniority, the farther back you sat. Players like Randy Carlyle, Mario Marios, and Serge Savard could ride "tailpipe" if they liked.

In his rookie year, Teemu Selanne sat in the seat right behind Don Wittman and me. On the way to the skate one morning, Teemu asked, "Guys, what's this Lady Byng trophy?" He had been hearing that he was a candidate to win it. When Witt and I explained it was for "gentlemanly conduct," Teemu got a glazed look on his face. He then began to collect penalties because, "it would have been embarrassing to win that award."

I Hear You Knocking, but You Can't Come In

THE FINAL GAME OF the '92–'93 season didn't mean a thing in terms of standings. The Winnipeg Jets had secured a playoff berth against Vancouver, while the Edmonton Oilers had long since been eliminated. Yet there was great excitement at the Winnipeg Arena, and it again centered on Teemu Selanne. Could the Jet who'd smashed the rookie goal-scoring record also win the league goal-scoring title? Selanne had seventy-five goals, Alexander Mogilny of the Buffalo Sabres had seventy-four. The Sabres closed at home that night as well against the Philadelphia Flyers.

Normally the Public Address announcer doesn't follow goal for goal what goes on at another rink, but this night was different; it was all about Selanne and Mogilny. Part way through the first period, PA announcer Kim Camarta announced, "Word from Buffalo, Alexander Mogilny has scored his seventy-fifth goal." A groan came from the crowd; Mogilny had caught Selanne. A few minutes later, "Selanne...scores number seventy-six!" The crowd went crazy. However, the celebration was short lived. "Word from Buffalo, Alexander Mogilny has scored again, his seventy-sixth." Again, the collective groan. Sometime later, another announcement, "Word from Buffalo, the game is over; Alexander Mogilny finished with seventy-six goals."

Thus, Selanne needed one to be the undisputed goal-scoring champion. Late in the third period, the stage was set. The Oilers took back-to-back penalties in short order. The crowd rose to its feet as number thirteen took his place on the power play. The puck stayed in the Oiler's end for the entire five on three. The Jets however were of single-purpose: get the puck and feed Selanne. Selanne would shoot, and goalie Bill Ranford would save.

What was learned that night is that Bill Ranford wasn't deaf. The Oiler netminder was among the thousands who heard the PA announcements. He knew that power play was all about Selanne, all about one last goal. It got to the point where Ranford squared to Selanne no matter who had the puck. At one stage, Alexei Zhamnov had the puck in the crease, and Ranford ignored him. Zhamnov pulled the puck back, passed to Selanne, and Ranford made the save. Thinking back, it was pretty funny, but nobody was laughing.

As it turned out there was no scoring at all in that third period. The Jets beat the Oilers 3–0 and Selanne finished tied with Mogilny for the goal-scoring title.

Buffalo won the two games between the Jets and Sabres that season, 6–2 and 2–1. Mogilny scored six of the Sabres eight goals.

Peanut Butter Night

NOV 5TH OF 1992 was "Peanut Butter" night at the Winnipeg Arena. Every fan was given a jar of peanut butter upon entering the building. The visitors were the lowly Ottawa Senators. It was their second season in the league, and they weren't very good. They were a team the Jets had to beat to stay in a playoff hunt.

Late in the game, the Jets appeared in control with a 6–4 lead. Then, at 18:12, Ottawa's Dave Archibald scored to make it 6–5. The crowd began to mumble. Moments later, the mumbling turned to grumbling when Bob Kudelski tied it to force overtime.

Then the unthinkable; Kudelski struck again! The mumbling and grumbling turned to rumbling, and airborne jars of peanut butter came tumbling to the ice! Hundreds, maybe a thousand of them! The goalies hid in their nets; players, coaches, and officials raced for cover! The ice was a mess, bathed end to end in unsightly brown lumps. It looked like the rodeo had been through.

Nobody was hurt, but ever after, "freebies" were handed out at the exits. The next morning in an effort to short-circuit the embarrassment, the Jets made a move. They stripped Dean Kennedy of the captaincy and gave the "C" to Keith Tkachuk.

Different Breed of Cat

IN FORMER JETS GENERAL manager Mike Smith, what you saw was what you got; there was no pretence. If he had bad news, he would not sugar coat it. He was a loner who wasn't concerned in the least about social acceptance. He abhorred small talk. If you were outside on a clear, warm summer day and said "nice day," he would ignore you. If, however, you asked about the goings-on in Cambodia or the floods in Florida or about the Jets power play, Doctor Smith with his PhD could talk forever. Smith danced to the beat of his own drummer, so when he showed up at the press conference called to announce his firing, it wasn't that much of a surprise; it was just Mike being Mike. He did, however, have something he wanted off his chest.

Smith's apparent infatuation with Russian hockey players was often discussed in Winnipeg, and he resented it. He referred to Winnipeg journalists as bigots for what he perceived to be an anti-Russian slant.

So, where did Mike go when he left the press conference? He went overseas alone to ride a train for two weeks: the Trans -Siberian Express through the heart of Russia.

I Don't See Any Stars

COACH JOHN PADDOCK TOOK pains to divert attention away from name players. When Teemu Selanne scored four goals but wasn't on the ice when Minnesota pulled their goaltender, he said it was because "Teemu didn't play very well." Whenever Bob Essensa played particularly well, Paddock would say, "He's paid to stop the puck." One day he called the media aside and asked that we quit interviewing Tie Domi altogether. On another occasion, I was at ice level introducing the Jet players individually when Paddock came over and whispered, "Don't introduce Teemu last." He was concerned about jealousy in the dressing room and there was always some of that.

As far as deflecting praise from Essensa, it was most notable in a year when Goalie Bob's contract was about to expire. I believe Paddock was under orders to downplay the performance of his goaltender.

A Burned Manitoba Bridge

IN 1993, COACH AND General Manager John Paddock enlisted Andy Murray as his number one assistant coach. It appeared to be a good fit with a nice local feel. Both were small-town western Manitoba boys, Paddock from tiny Oak River and Murray from Souris. There was an understanding (possibly an agreement) that eventually, Paddock would remove himself as head coach, and Murray would move in.

However, when the transition didn't happen, it was a surprise to no one. Players and media saw it coming from miles away. The Jets had brought in another highly qualified assistant coach in Terry Simpson, who had suddenly become Paddock's "go-to guy." Paddock would ride on the front seat of the team bus contemplating strategy, and when he needed a second opinion, he would summon Simpson to join him, while Andy Murray sat alone in the seat behind them, and seethed. He had become the coaching equivalent of a spare tire.

Eventually, in 1995, with the Jets in the throes of a ten-game winless streak, Paddock removed himself as coach and elevated Terry Simpson. Murray felt betrayed and left in a huff.

In later years however, things worked out; Murray went on to be the longest serving head coach in the history of the Los Angeles Kings.

Six More Weeks of This?

THE '93–'94 JETS HAD been expected to fly high but instead went into a nosedive. Losses piled up to the point that on Feb 2nd (Groundhog Day), goalie Bob Essensa was booed before the game even started, when he accepted the "player of the month" award. The fans were "mad as hell and weren't going to take it anymore."

It was much worse than anything we'd seen in the thirty-game winless season. The earlier team was short on talent, but this group featured Teemu Selanne, Keith Tkachuk, Alexei Zhamnov, all in their second seasons. They also had Thomas Steen, Nelson Emerson and Teppo Nummenin; they were supposed to be good. However, they didn't win from mid-January to early March, a nineteen-game winless streak that was made up of sixteen losses and three ties.

The highlight of that lost season was March 2nd, and it wasn't because the streak finally ended. The highlight was the reaction to the win. The same fans who'd booed the Jets a month earlier, gave them a standing ovation. It was a bittersweet moment that defined the term "faithful fans."

It's Your Fault!

IN 1995, WHEN IT became clear that the Jets were leaving Winnipeg, there were hard feelings all around. Everyone pointed a finger of blame: some at the owners, some at the players, some at the antiquated Winnipeg Arena, some at the city fathers, and some at Americans for "kidnapping our game." There were in fact, many reasons, including the devalued Canadian dollar. Some desperate fans thought the government should come to the rescue. But what government could justify a bail-out package to a business that paid one employee (Keith Tkachuk) the equivalent of 8 million Canadian a year?

Another irritant to fans was Gary Bettman's countenance. Whether he means to or not, the Commissioner often wears a "sneer," a trait that makes him look uppity and uncaring. He became the villain in the eyes of many. (He was often compared unfavourably with the Count from Sesame Street.)

The fans were fed up with all of it, and many withdrew their support prior to the final season. Understandable, why would you invest emotionally and financially in a love that will soon be lost?

Selling Borrowed Time

KNOWING IN ADVANCE THAT a team is leaving is a marketing nightmare; it's the ultimate turn-off for fans. Early in the final season, the indifference was evident. Crowd counts of 9,000 were common at the Winnipeg Arena. However, everybody circled one date on the calendar, April 12, 1996. It was to be the final home game, and it sold out seven months in advance.

When the day arrived, there was an added bonus; a win would secure a playoff berth. 15,567 people showed up clad in white, and the Jets did not disappoint them. Craig Janney scored two goals, and Keith Tkachuk netted his fiftieth in a 5–3 win over the Los Angeles Kings.

The Jets were playoff bound and may even start the post season at home! Euphoria had returned to Winnipeg, if only temporarily.

Sad Reality

MOST EVERYONE HAS SEEN the video of the original Jets farewell, the chants, the tears, and Eddy Olczyk's pledge to "bring the Stanley Cup back to Winnipeg!" But there was something else, something the cameras missed.

Well after the game ended and most of the 15,000 plus had filed out, I went back into the arena bowl and was stunned by what I saw. There was a smattering of people, some of them seated, some of them on the ice, all eerily quiet, and it appeared that *every single one was a teen-aged boy*. They were staring as if in shock. There was no macho, no bravado, just real tears.

These young guys were feeling the pain like no other; they had been let down. The Jets had been around all their lives; many had dreamed of being a Jet one day. For some who'd not yet experienced the loss of a loved one, this was as close as they had come. Reality had reared its ugly head.

Teased

AFTER THAT LAST GAME, there was a final flicker of hope that the Jets would stay. The "Save the Jets" campaign was an awesome sight; it seemed to involve everyone in Manitoba and beyond. People with no interest in hockey were as caught up as the rest of us. The Jets were going to stay; they had to stay! The heart ruled. Many people vowed financial support beyond their means.

Hope reached a high point after a party at former Jet Thomas Steen's house. Many well-to-do people were there and pledged financial involvement. They also phoned wealthy former Manitobans and got them to commit. It seemed like it could happen, but in the end, it was too good to be true. Even the indelible image of children smashing their piggy banks and offering all they had wasn't enough to sway the richest of the rich, and the dream died.

On the Brink

WHEN SOMETHING BIG IS about to happen with hockey in Winnipeg, the corner of Portage and Main becomes the focal point.

It started in 1972 with an appearance by Bobby Hull, Ben Hatskin, and a giant cheque for an unheard of one million dollars. It solidified the credibility of the WHA and Winnipeg's major pro-inclusion. In 1981, a Brinks truck arrived at the same intersection carrying Dale Hawerchuk. It signified the Jets were going to be a very real player on the NHL stage.

Unfortunately, Portage and Main was also the sight of a false alarm. In 1996 thousands of people abandoned work or skipped school, expecting to hear that the Winnipeg Jets had been saved in a last-ditch effort. But we had all been fooled. The announcement didn't come, and a raucous party turned to a funeral dirge, complete with tears.

It was eleven years until the next Jets inspired get-together at the iconic corner. A spontaneous eruption of joy at the news the Atlanta Thrashers were coming to Winnipeg and coming to stay!

Quotes and Denials

SHORTLY AFTER HIS WHA Jets had won a game on the road, playing Coach Bobby Hull announced a curfew "Anyone caught in his room before 2 a.m. won't play tomorrow night!"

Upon returning to Winnipeg from an international tournament, Hull's Swedish linemate Ulf Nilsson was asked what was wrong with the Swedish national team? His response, "Too many Swedes."

With his team in the throes of their thirty-game winless streak, a reporter asked Coach Tom McVie if he was having any trouble sleeping? The baritone McVie growled, "I sleep like a baby, every two hours, I wake up crying."

In the early '80s, the New York Islanders were the cream of the crop. Thus, when the hapless 1980 Jets played them to a tie, Coach Al Arbour was livid. He stormed out of the dressing room to the assembled media and with fire in his eyes blurted, "I've got nothing to say, and I'm only going to say it once!" He then verbally fried every player on his team, before pivoting and slamming the dressing room door.

Tom Watt trumpeted the "fact" that he never read a newspaper. A sentiment echoed by many of his peers, including Tom McVie and Bob Murdoch. Thus, it was a constant source of amazement how each knew exactly what was written about them.

One day in Toronto, I boarded the hotel elevator to go down and catch the team bus to the Jets/Leafs game. I was joined on the elevator by a couple with game tickets in hand. We began talking, and I learned that they were the parents of that night's referee, Andy Van Hellemond. I suggested that they would be the only people there cheering for the referee. Mr. Van Hellemond's retort: "No, we hate referees too."

In 1988 the Los Angeles Kings beat the Jets 2–1 thanks to a scintillating goaltending performance. Postgame, we spoke to the winning goalie who used the term "you know" thirty-six times in a forty-five-second answer. The goalie, Glenn Healy, went on to become a successful network broadcaster.

After an Oiler loss in Winnipeg, Oiler Esa Tikkanen was chosen one of the three stars. He told us postgame, "I'm proud of the Jets; they played well. I'm glad they won."

Pavol Krc was a Czech defector who joined the Jets training camp in 1979. After a couple of days, he was cut and ever after referred to as the "defective Czech."

A guy named Sullivan arrived at Jets camp with long hair, a guitar, and beads and insisted on a tryout. He was cut when he stepped on the ice wearing sandals.

Kirk McCaskill tried out for the Jets. When that didn't work out, he went south and pitched twelve seasons for the California Angels and Chicago White Sox.

You're a Pig Blondie! (A quote from the movie: *The Good, the Bad and the Ugly*.)

Some players shoot the puck every chance they get; Alexander Ovechkin is the prime example, so was Brett Hull and, presumably, Rocket Richard. Others have a pass-first mentality. Former Jet Bengt Lundholm once instinctively took the puck off the opposition goal line and fed it out front to a teammate whose shot missed the net. Jet great, Thomas Steen was another who preferred to spread the wealth. One night at the Winnipeg Arena, Steen scored twice before the game was three minutes old, then on his next shift, he passed rather than slide it into an empty net. By my count, Steen should have easily scored four in that first period alone. The next day I asked the humble Swede why he didn't cash those in. He replied, "I didn't want to be a hog."

Not "Just Another Game"

DURING THE COURSE OF every season, there's a game or two with special meaning. It might be the battle to decide first place or even the seventh game of a playoff series. That's inevitably when players and coaches will drone on about it being "just another game." Everyone knows it's not. The fans clamour for this kind of setting. They simply want their team to admit there's a lot on the line, but instead they drag it down. It's amazing that players, coaches, and even management can be such poor salesmen for their sport.

Coach Bob Murdoch was in a league of his own in that regard. Prior to game seven between his Jets and the Edmonton Oilers, I used the old "must-win" line to begin our pregame interview. His reply, "Well, I wouldn't call it a must-win, but obviously if we lose, we go home."

It's a good thing he's not a heart surgeon.

Humble Servants

DUE TO HIS RELIGIOUS convictions, Jets netminder Joe
Daley became known as the "Holy Goalie," but he wasn't
alone. It was a moniker that could have just as easily been
worn by later Jets goaltender Eddie Staniowski, or in particular by Dan Bouchard. Bouchard prefaced every public
comment by praising God. His reaction to playing well
was always, "Lord be praised!"

It made me curious as to how he would react after a bad
game. When the situation presented itself, I approached
him, microphone in hand and asked, "What happened?"

His answer, "The Lord likes to humble me once in
a while."

Awkward Moment

IN MY FIRST YEAR, I was asked to do an interview with the
coach of the Quebec Nordiques. I said, "Sure, no problem,"
but there was a problem. While I knew the coach's name,
I had no idea what he looked like. Then opportunity
struck, a slight, well- dressed man showed up at the visi-
tor's bench in the Winnipeg Arena. He had to be affiliated
with the Nordiques. I asked, "Excuse me, can you tell me
where I can find, Michel Bergeron, the coach?" He looked
at me, paused, then proudly proclaimed, "I...am Michel
Bergeron...the coach." A stunned silence followed as the

conversation echoed through the hollows of my mind, then I began to laugh, and so did he. I remember thinking afterward that it was a good thing it was Bergeron I was unable to identify; someone like Glen Sather would not have been amused.

Nicknames

MOST ATHLETE'S NICKNAMES ARE predictable and ho-hum. Add an "er" or an "sy," and it's your handle forever: Doaner, Jonesy. Some names though do have imagination.

Former Jets captain Dave Christian was "Coma" because his was a different world. The same could be said for Freddy "The Fog" Olausson. Randy Carlyle was "Kitty" and the teammates he hung around with, like Peter Taglianetti, Phil Housley, and Randy Gilhen, became the "Kitty Litter." There was Barry "Buzzard" Long and Ian "Slam" Duncan. Goaltenders Eldon Reddick and Daniel Berthiaume were "Pokey and the Bandit."

Brian Mullen was "Moon," Dale Hawerchuk was "Ducky," Peter Sullivan was "Spud," Ron Wilson was "Dawg," Teppo Nummenin was "Repo." If you ever wondered why Dave Ellet was called "Roy," it's because John Ferguson referred to him as a "natural." There was a movie out at that time called *The Natural* and the central figure was a baseball player named Roy Hobbs.

An early Jets defenceman, Al Cameron, had his conditioning level called into question and came to be known as "Sluggo." Hard working Bill Lesuk was "Tractor." Wade

Campbell, who towered over everybody, became "Tree," and his defence partner Tim Watters was "Muddy."

There was well-travelled Gary "Suitcase" Smith. Thomas Steen briefly became "Woodstock" after a tattoo of the creature appeared mysteriously on his backside. Tom Martin came to the Jets with his nickname firmly in place. He was called "Bus." In his junior days, Martin's team traded him for a bus. Dave Manson had a fearsome reputation that earned him the nickname "Charlie" (as in Manson).

Even broadcasters earned nicknames: Ken Nicolson was better known as "Friar." I got lost in the Atlanta airport in my rookie season, and ever after was "Sod," as in sodbuster from Saskatchewan.

There were others who had titles rather than nicknames. Goalie Nikolai Khabibulin was "The Bulin Wall," and muscle-bound Sean Cronin became "Cronin the Barbarian." Teemu Selanne was the "Finnish Flash" and Alexei Zhamnov, the "Red-headed Russian." And let us not forget "The Golden Jet" Bobby Hull.

What heritage?

WHEN IS A RETIRED number not a retired number? When it's retired by the Winnipeg Jets apparently. When Jets 2 came along they immediately doled out the number nine jersey to Evander Kane. When he left, they gave it to Andrew Kopp.

They will never do that in Chicago.

Quiet Loser!

WHEN YOU WALK INTO a dressing room after a win, the music is playing, and there's plenty of laughter. Star players are being interviewed while others do their utmost to distract them with hijinks.

After a loss, the room is deathly quiet. The players who agree to be interviewed speak in such hushed tones that the interviewer often doesn't have a clue what they're saying. In the early days, that period of quiet would carry over to the bus ride to the hotel or airport. The postgame pout was mandatory. A period of supposed self-loathing when if anyone dared speak aloud, a glare or an expletive- filled tirade would come from the coach or General Manager riding in the front seat.

On New Year's Eve 1979, the first-year Jets had just lost a close game to a pretty good team in Buffalo. The Jets had played well. On the ride to Toronto after the game, a chorus was struck up on the back of the bus. Players began to join in; it was Auld Lang Syne. It seemed so refreshing. At least until the sound carried to the front of the bus and the baritone voice of coach Tom McVie growled, "Shut up! You don't sing when you lose!" Welcome to 1980.

In later years the postgame pout hasn't been as prevalent. Players and sometimes even coaches don't take every loss like a death in the family. I'm not sure why, although it could have something to do with cell phones. A lot of players like to call home after a game, and It's tough speaking quietly when on a bus and calling Russia.

Oleg Tverdovsky's dad must have been near deaf.

Above the Rest

SOME PLAYERS HAVE "COURAGE of conviction," others tend to cower when times get tough. The Jets always had a few guys you could talk to under any circumstance. Paul MacLean comes to mind, so does Laurie Boschman, Robert Picard, Morris Lukowich, and Dave Ellet. Keith Tkachuk and Shane Doan were there to answer the bell in Phoenix.

One group that always hid after a loss was the Vancouver Canucks. You'd get to the dressing room and see the equipment guys, the media, and Stan Smyl. Smyl was the captain of the Canucks and the ultimate stand-up guy. One time after a Canuck win, I went to the dressing room and noted all the media gathered around Tony Tanti, who'd scored a hat trick that night. I steered clear and headed to Smyl, who was seated alone. He asked why I wanted to speak with him? I said, "I thought you might want the pleasure of speaking after a win." He immediately knew what I meant, laughed, and gave me a great interview.

One group of players was actually hard to find after a home win. The Edmonton Oilers liked to gather in a backroom, pile on each other like cordwood and marvel over the replays of their goals.

91

Who's Number One?

KEITH TKACHUK WAS PROUD to a fault; he had to be the biggest dog in the park. If he was convinced in his own mind that he was the team's best player, he thrived. If he felt competition for the mantle, he could be sullen. In the wake of a celebration of a Teemu Selanne milestone goal, TV cameras panned the bench, and Tkachuk was seen forming the words, "Just get the *#%!*ing game going!"

When the Jets abandoned Winnipeg and landed in Phoenix, Tkachuk was front and centre; it was his team. Then, the Coyotes made a splash by signing Jeremy Roenick. The territorial Tkachuk felt threatened once again. However, after a few weeks, it became obvious to all, including the captain, that he was still king of the hill. With his self-confidence restored, Tkachuk accepted Roenick, and the two became good teammates and better friends.

Tkachuk was admired by some, disliked by others. He could be accommodating to fans and media or he could be dismissive. If you supported him, he was extremely generous, as a lot of therapists and equipment handlers in the league would attest. He would bark at them and demand obedience; then, at season's end, he would make it all worthwhile. A previous Jets leader was much the same in that latter regard, Randy Carlyle.

Both Tkachuk and Carlyle have crusty exteriors but soft underbellies. Several local charities will attest to that.

Cool and Cocky

JEREMY ROENICK HAS A personality more akin to an NFL wide receiver than a hockey player. He never ventures far from the spotlight. He's flamboyant in his colourful clothes and hot cars, complete with personalised license plates (JR-97). He had the nickname "Styles" inscribed on his hockey sticks. When most of the Coyotes lived in upscale Scottsdale, Roenick one-bettered them by living in Paradise Valley.

He's exceptionally bold, as was evidenced on his first road trip with the Coyotes. On the way home, he ventured where no player dares go uninvited. He went to the front of the charter plane and presented the new owners Richard Burke and Steven Gluckstern with a bottle of Dom Perignon, then proceeded to share it with them.

While his new teammates stared in disbelief, Roenick remained cool. In his mind, he's never out of bounds.

Committed

WHEN TEAMS ARE PLAYING poorly, they'll often call a "players only" meeting intended to resolve things and get back to winning. Sometimes these meetings are "rah rah," other times, they get personal; everyone has a chance to vent. People presume the captains do the talking but not always. Brian Sutter once blasted Wayne Gretzky, Mark Messier, Ray Bourque, and a host of other big names in the intermission of an exhibition game prior to a Canada Cup tournament. Sutter had no hesitation in speaking his mind even though as it turned out, he didn't make the team. That team did go on to win the 1984 Canada Cup.

You don't have to wear the "C" to be a leader. Randy Carlyle was a classic example in Winnipeg, as was Serge Savard, although his time in Winnipeg was short.

Goaltenders too can lead, although they can't wear the "C" anymore. Sean Burke was the E.F. Hutton of the Coyotes. He blasted Keith Tkachuk and Jeremy Roenick after a lopsided loss in Montreal. On another occasion, he hollered after a game, "Get some guys who can play!" He'd tended goal that night in St. Louis where the Coyotes were beaten 2–1 and outshot forty-five to nineteen. He said teams that can't win on the road have no heart.

It takes courage and conviction to speak out like Sutter and Burke. By dropping the gauntlet, they expose themselves to ridicule if they're less than the best they can be every night.

Gotcha

THEO FLEURY OF THE Calgary Flames was worth the price of admission. He was an entertainer with great talent and an incredible knack for getting under the skin of opponents and fans alike. He was a pest. Opposing players couldn't do a whole lot about it either. Due to Fleury's diminutive stature, if you pummeled him, you were seen as a bully, plus you'd have to answer to a very big and very surly bunch of Calgary Flames.

Jets goaltender Rick Tabaracci found that out the hard way. He stepped out of his net and slammed into Fleury in a game in Winnipeg. The hit drew a standing ovation. However, the teams met again two days later, and early in the first period Flames Gary Roberts took a fearsome run at Tabaracci.

Late one season, the Flames and Jets played a key game in Calgary. The score was 3–3 with ten minutes left when Fleury went down on the ice writhing in agony. Jet Brent Ashton was assessed a five-minute spearing penalty. Fleury stayed down for several minutes. He was helped to the bench, and when he got there, he began laughing. He hadn't been hurt at all. The Jets were able to weather the five-minute disadvantage only to lose 4–3 in overtime. And to rub it in, the overtime goal was scored by Fleury, and he laughed again.

Mixed Bag of
Random and Silly

WHY DO HOCKEY TEAMS encourage fans to applaud and shout their support, then when the home team scores and their enthusiasm crescendos, drown them out with a horn?

Plus-Minus is often guilt by association. If your two linemates were Gretzky and Kurri, would you be a minus? It's like someone once said, "A minus is like giving the right fielder an error because the shortstop dropped the ball."

The term "game-winning goal" conjures up an image of late-game heroics, but if you take a big lead and your opponent rallies to lose 4–3, the game-winning goal was the one that made it 4–0. It was window dressing.

Winnipeg Jets goalie Mike O'Neal finished the '93–'94 season with a record of 0–9–1 and was named the team's rookie of the year.

When a team is getting soundly beaten you can count on a broadcaster saying, "There's no quit in this team!" Really, should there be? Does the plumber leave when the toilet's overflowing?

Or "distractions." When there's an ownership financial fiasco, you'll hear about how a team is coping admirably despite the distractions. Do they really think when a player is staring in from the point on the power play, he's wondering how his owner is making out at the Swiss bank?

While we're at it, what's with "flu-like symptoms?" Why not say the player has the flu? It is a relative term.

You can always tell which athlete has watched one too many hero movies. He's the one that, after his team has won a championship, will say, "Nobody believed in us, everyone counted us out, but we never doubted ourselves."

On any given night, you can tune into a hockey or basketball broadcast and hear the analyst marvel over what he calls an "unselfish" play. It's often when a player ignores a scoring opportunity to make a needless pass. It's not "unselfish" at all; it's just a bad play and should never draw praise. The true unselfish play is to score the goal; that is what benefits the team the most. Quell the trumpet.

Was Carlyle Cream or Sour Milk?

ON MARCH 9TH, 1988, the Winnipeg Jets and Calgary Flames played to a 6–6 tie. Jets defenceman Randy Carlyle had five points and wound up minus four. His goal and four assists all came on the power play.

Be Careful What You Wish For

THE TERM "PARITY" CAN leave the wrong impression. Parity is a salary ceiling designed to put all teams on an equal footing. It's a way for small market teams to compete with the likes of New York, Los Angeles, Chicago, and Toronto. But parity should never find its way to the ice. Nobody wants to see a bunch of teams playing 500 hockey and a different Stanley Cup winner every year.

Sports fans need a team to revile as much as they need a team to cheer for. "Disdain" has to be earned and winning championships will do that. There's a reason the networks carry more New England Patriots games than Jacksonville Jaguars. Fans thrive on love/hate relationships. In hockey, does anyone hate the Winnipeg Jets or Arizona Coyotes? And it'll be that way until one or the other wins it all.

The rise and fall of dynasties is a good thing. The Montreal Canadiens, the New York Islanders, and the Edmonton Oilers among others, have taken turns at being the game's greatest draw.

Parity should never breed mediocrity.

Bite the Hand That Feeds

WHEN THE EDMONTON OILERS won their first Stanley Cup in 1984, they scored 446 goals in an eighty-game season (5.5 per game.) A lot of people watched. When the New Jersey Devils won the cup in 2003, they scored less than half that amount (216 goals in eighty-two games.) Fewer people watched.

Hockey fans are best served when the neutral zone is a runway, not a gathering spot.

Goalposts

SOME OF THE BEST and worst deals are the ones that aren't made. The Stars nearly traded Mike Modano to the Jets for Phil Housley. The Jets nearly drafted Cam Neely, then at the last moment opted for Andrew McBain. The Coyotes nearly got Joe Thornton from Boston; when they hesitated, he went to San Jose.

In the late '70s, the Winnipeg Jets were given first dibs on Wayne Gretzky, but General Manager Rudy Pilous thought he was too skinny, so Nelson Skalbania and the Indianapolis Racers sold him to Peter Pocklington in Edmonton.

Born on the Wagon of a Travelin' Show

WHY WOULD ANY NEW or transplanted franchise debut on the road? The original Jets played their first game in Pittsburgh; the Coyotes opened in Hartford. At least Jets 2 got it right: they played their first game at home.

People get excited when their town is awarded a franchise; they count the days until the season opener. They deserve the first look. Why should a total stranger unwrap their gift? It's goofy; even the entertainment capital of the world saw its franchise start elsewhere. The Las Vegas Golden Knights premiered in Dallas. Then there's the Seattle Kraken who really blew it; they opened with five games on the road. The first time their fans saw them, they were near last place. A new franchise should debut like a newborn baby, near family and friends.

The Regal Touch

ROOKIE INITIATIONS (HAZINGS) HAVE been going on forever. The late Pat Quinn figured Plato was probably hazed at one time. A common hazing practice is to have a few players hold a rookie down and shave his nether regions. In 1980, the Winnipeg Jets tried that with Dave Babych, but it didn't work. The herculean teenager could not be held down by five or six mere mortals.

It was a good thing for opposition players that Babych was a friendly sort. I recall two occasions when he got upset and literally rag-dolled his prey. He picked each up with one hand and fired a blow with the other. He never needed a second punch.

One day at the Winnipeg Arena, the clean-up crew was surprised to have front row seats to an x rated show. The Toronto Maple Leafs were there for a practice and decided it was a "regal" place to initiate a rookie. Where else could you do it right in front of the Queen! So, they strapped the young player to a gurney and wheeled him to centre ice. Then they brought out the razor and performed the ritual ceremony, in full view of Her Majesty's image, and the highly entertained sanitation engineers.

The Winnipeg Arena had a humongous picture of Queen Elizabeth II that dominated one end of the building. At practice, players would often compete to see if anyone could flip the puck high enough to impact royalty. A smattering of black smears was a testament to some level of success.

No Ringy-Dingy

DURING TRAINING CAMP, YOU could always count on getting a good laugh from a rookie.

The Jets were in Vancouver when one young Einstein figured out how to beat curfew. He smuggled the hotel's phone from his room and took it to his girlfriend's house. He would simply answer it there and claim to be in his room. But oddly, the hotel's phone didn't ring at her place. He was on a plane home to America the next morning.

Then there was the young goaltender from Quebec who was shocked he didn't have to clear Customs to go from Winnipeg to Vancouver.

A Kingdom for a Knockout Punch!

THE WINNIPEG JETS ELIMINATED the Calgary Flames in the playoffs in 1987. It took the franchise twenty-five years to win another series. The Phoenix Coyotes had success in 2012. Some years they didn't make the postseason, and sometimes they were eliminated in short order, then there were the others. A cruel and unusual litany of others.

On twelve occasions the Jets/Coyotes needed one win to advance to the next round, they lost all twelve games. In 1990 Dave Ellet scored in double-overtime to give the

Jets a 3–1 series lead, but the Edmonton Oilers won the next three games, and ultimately the Stanley Cup.

Two years later the Jets took a 3–1 series lead over Vancouver, then got blown out of the water. In the last three games they were outscored 21 to 5.

The franchise moved but the teasing continued. The first year Phoenix Coyotes blew a 3–2 series lead against the Mighty Ducks of Anaheim. Two years later they squandered a 3–1 series lead against St. Louis. Add to that a seventh game loss to Detroit in 2010, and you have it, 0 for 12. 0 for a quarter century.

Rivered

JAMIE RIVERS WAS THE ultimate "specialist" in that playoff series between St. Louis and Phoenix. He ONLY played the power play. Thus, when he made a series changing defensive play, the writing was on the wall.

The Coyotes had a chance to wrap it in game five at home. They had a 1–0 third period lead when Keith Tkachuk got a shorthanded breakaway. His shot trickled between the pads of goalie Grant Fuhr and was about to cross the goal line when Rivers dove headlong, and swatted the puck away. It eventually wound up on the stick of Al MacInnes whose power play goal forced over-time, and a Blues win.

Hodge Podge

WHO'D HAVE THOUGHT THAT one of the most memorable moments in the history of Jets 1 was a goal that ultimately didn't change anything? All Jets fans of the day remember where they were when Dave Ellet scored his double-overtime goal. It gave the Jets a 3–1 series lead over the hated Oilers, but the Oilers went on to win the Stanley Cup anyway, while the Jets never won again that year.

It took the NHL a while to realize how popular and eventful the first round of the playoffs could be. In the early '80s, it seemed they couldn't wait to get the first round over with. It was a best of five and had to be completed in a week. A typical scenario: they would play Wednesday and Thursday at the home of the higher seed, travel Friday for another set of back- to-backs Saturday and Sunday, then travel Monday for the deciding game Tuesday. As the coach said in the hockey movie *Goon*, "This isn't *%#@ing baseball!"

Talk about a rough start. The Jets season opener in '89–'90 was at home, where they scored four goals in the first period and three of them were disallowed. They lost that game 4–1 to John Vanbiesbrouck and the New York Rangers. Replays revealed that two of the three disallowed goals should have counted. It wasn't referee Mark Faucette's best day.

Short-term St. Louis Blue, Paul Skidmore knows all about rough starts. When Jet Doug Smail scored five seconds from the start of the game, Skidmore was making his NHL goaltending debut.

When you're on the beat and a new head coach comes in, you never know what to expect. Will the coach be approachable, even social, or will be a miserable S.O.B.? The latter seemed like such a waste to me. These were people who had achieved dream jobs yet dealt with them like they were slopping hogs, unsmiling and owly. The only certainties in coaching are that you're going to win some, you're going to lose some, and you're going to be fired; so, enjoy the ride. I must admit though, I was fortunate in that regard, most of the coaches and managers I dealt with were easy to get along with, some became good friends.

A lot of coaches, even some players who came to Winnipeg or Phoenix from eastern markets, came armed with paranoia. Coach Dan Maloney was a prime example. When he got to Winnipeg from Toronto, he looked at the media with disdain. He didn't trust any of us. He even forbade his assistant coaches from socializing with us on the road. (An edict that was ignored.) However, after a while he realized we weren't all pariahs bent on his destruction, and good times followed.

Still with Maloney, in 1989, his job was on the line. The Jets were considered "under achievers" which is a fancy term for blame the coach. Maloney became aware that there was to be a story in the *Winnipeg Free Press* the next day stating that he and captain Dale Hawerchuk were feuding. Maloney knew that if ownership accepted the story at face value, he'd be fired. He asked Pat Doyle of the *Winnipeg Sun* and me to interview him, at which time he vehemently denied any disharmony between he and his captain. We then went to Hawerchuk, and while he didn't give his coach a ringing endorsement, he didn't shove him under the bus either. Maloney was very appreciative, but to no avail, he was fired a month later.

Allow Me

IN THE FALL OF 1988, when Winnipeg's Donny Lalonde fought Sugar Ray Leonard for the light heavyweight boxing championship, the Winnipeg Jets had a free night in Quebec City. The garçon at the hotel made arrangements for some of us to see the fight at a local watering hole.

The fight was on a double screen with no sound; it was a pirated feed. With the left eye you'd see a dancing Sugar Ray being stalked by the "Golden Boy," while the right eye was witnessing a ménage à trois. One person with us was a lady; she sat with her back to the screen.

The staff at La Brasserie was excited to see Dan Maloney there. They knew he coached the Jets and that they were in town to challenge the Nordiques the next night. They could not have been more obliging. Every second round of quarts was on the house.

Eventually then, nature called and the young lady in our company had to answer. That's when we realized there were no other women in the bar; it was a men's club. Had we not been in the company of an NHL coach, we'd have not been allowed in. What was she to do? There was no ladies' room.

Dan Maloney seized control. The rugged coach waded into the washroom and in a matter of seconds a half dozen male patrons scurried out, jabbering in mixed languages. Maloney then stood guard at the washroom entrance with his arms crossed like a cigar store fixture and politely said to the lady, "You can go in there now, miss."

Vote, Vote, Vote for the Home Team

I'VE NEVER BEEN A fan of ballot box stuffing. People are encouraged to vote a thousand times for their favourite player in order to get him some all-star recognition. It happens in all sports.

The NHL was forced to make a small alteration after the 2016 All-Star game when John Scott of the St. John's Ice Caps was voted in. Really, by the rules of the day, Rocket Richard could have been voted in posthumously.

When someone gets in who doesn't belong, it follows that someone is left out. A classic example of that occurred in 1991. Halfway through the season goalie Eddie Belfour of the Black Hawks personally had more wins than any other team in the NHL, yet he was overlooked for the All-Star game. The fans voted in Mike Vernon, and the coach, John Muckler of the Oilers, refused to leave the farm and named Oilers goalie Bill Ranford as the second teamer.

To make it worse, the All-Star game was in Chicago.

Get a Life

THE "THREE STAR" SELECTION is an outdated thankless task that serves little purpose. You're damned if you do and damned if you don't pick "Johnny" as a star. The amazing thing to me was often the reaction of a coach or general manager. They'd be heard to holler, "Who the hell picked those stars?" It seemed to me they had more pressing concerns, particularly if their club had lost. If their club had won, shouldn't they be happy?

The worst I ever saw was January 19, 1983. The Winnipeg Jets had scored a 6–3 home-ice victory over the Toronto Maple Leafs. The Jets "Tre Kroner" line had dominated the game; there was never an easier choice of three stars. Former WHA Jet Dunc Rousseau was tasked with the selection that night. His stars were #1 Thomas Steen, #2 Willie Lindstrom and #3 Bengt Lundholm. Perfect! However, when the stars were announced to the crowd, Steen was not among them, instead Rick Vaive of the Leafs was slotted in.

The crowd became angry and the target of their disgust was Rousseau, but it wasn't his fault. It was a Toronto TV executive who made the change. He felt that because the game was being televised to Toronto, it was mandatory that at least one star be a Leaf.

It was bad, but what was even worse is that Rousseau received threats after that. Some people need to expand their world.

Stew's Stars

ONE YEAR, THE JETS decided the three stars should be selected by a committee of five people. Each of us would submit three names in order, and broadcaster Stew McPherson would tally the results.

There was, however, a problem. McPherson had to begin gathering ballots in the third period; you couldn't wait until the game was near an end to make your selection. A second problem, Mr. McPherson was of age and didn't move very quickly. It got to the point where he'd demand your ballot before the third period was half over. That doesn't work. If the score is 1–0 because a goaltender has been brilliant, then gives up two "softies," you're made to look like a fool. The Jets saw the error of their ways and abandoned that system after one season.

Say What?

IN THE JETS' FINAL season, rumours began circulating that Teemu Selanne would be traded. It bothered him. It was bad enough the team was leaving Winnipeg; he didn't want to leave the team too. Out of the blue he got a phone call from Coyotes Owner Richard Burke assuring him that he was a big part of the team's future in Phoenix.

Two weeks later, he was traded to Anaheim for Oleg Tverdovsky.

Hockey Town

I WAS INTERVIEWING BRYAN "Butsy" Erickson of the Jets, and I naively asked him when he began to realize that he was the best player in his small hometown. He replied, "Best player in town? I wasn't even the best player on my street!" Erickson is from Roseau, Minnesota; his neighbours were the Brotens. Neal, Aaron, and Paul Broten all played in the NHL.

Bearer of Bad Tidings

VALERI KHARLAMOV, ONE OF the greatest hockey players of all time, was killed in a car accident in Russia in the fall of 1981. At that precise time, the Soviet national team was in Winnipeg for a Canada Cup game. I gave a morning radio report on the tragedy and immediately afterward was called to the phone. It was Winnipegger Aggie Kukulowicz, who was serving as the interpreter for the Soviet team. The hockey team knew nothing of the tragedy and demanded to know the origin of the story. I went to the team headquarters at the Viscount Gort Hotel and told them what little I knew. They refused to believe me. They called the homeland, but no one would confirm what I had told them. It was an eerie feeling. A couple of players looked at me with "dagger- eyes." Unfortunately, it was true, and fortunately, they didn't shoot the messenger.

Valeri Kharlamov was incredible in the historic Summit Series between Canada and the Soviet Union in 1972. So much so that in game six, Team Canada Assistant Coach John Ferguson enlisted Bobby Clarke to, "Give Kharlamov a little tap on the ankle." Clarke complied on his next shift, which rendered Kharlamov unavailable for game seven, and ineffective in game eight. Serge Savard, who played in that series, ranked Kharlamov "one of the five greatest hockey players of all time."

To the Well and Back

IN THE LATE '80s, there was a lot of discontent on the Soviet national hockey team. Their coach, Viktor Tikhonov, had absolute control. He kept his team together and away from family for eleven months of the year. They lived on an army barracks and slept on cots. Some of the players had been drafted by NHL teams and wanted a taste of a better life. Tikhonov would have none of it. Eventually though, at great personal risk, Viacheslav Fetisov and Igor Larionov broke the door open and led a break to the promised land.

So, it's ironic that Viktor Tikhonov's grandson (who has the same name) went on to play for the Phoenix Coyotes, while Viacheslav Fetisov went back to Russia to work for Vladimir Putin.

Above Reproach

BEING AN OFFICIAL IN any sport is tough. How do football officials determine what is fair and what is foul in a game where there are numerous infractions on every play? Would you like to be one of those line judges in tennis who gets screamed at? Basketball players and their coaches whine over nearly every foul. How about the home plate umpire in a fourteen-inning game in stifling heat? Let us not forget the hockey referee. Cursed at if you do, and cursed at if you don't call a penalty late in a tie game. Years ago, that wasn't a problem. The referee would simply put his whistle away, particularly in playoff overtime, and the law of the jungle prevailed.

The NHL used to send a directive to broadcasters prior to the season, which said basically, "Lay off the officials, or there will be consequences." The consequences we found out a couple of times were simple phone calls saying, "You shouldn't oughta say that." That just worked in reverse, particularly for the likes of Ken "Friar" Nicolson, the original voice of the Jets. His theory was quite simple: if you can criticize players, coaches, general managers, and broadcasters, why can't you call out a referee?

A referee builds a psychological wall of resistance over time, and being booed by 15,000 people is just another night on the job. Looking at it from a distance, I think the toughest part of being an NHL on-ice official is the travel. It's okay if you're doing a game in New York one day and New Jersey the next, but what about the west? Where do you go from

Winnipeg or Denver? You go the airport and hang around for long boring hours. Meanwhile the players, coaches, team officials, and broadcasters have already arrived at the next port of call via charter. I remember Wayne Gretzky saying he couldn't understand why the referees and linesmen couldn't board the charter if they were going the same place anyway? I think it makes sense unless, of course, you question their integrity, in which case you shouldn't have hired them in the first place.

However, having said that, you would likely need to recruit Seal Team Six to get an official on any flight where Lou Lamoriello was in charge.

"Bear" Justice

BILL MACCREARY WAS ONE of the best referees in the NHL, but sometimes, like everyone else, he would miss a blatant penalty. One afternoon, at the Boston Garden, Winnipeg Jet Paul Fenton caught Bruin Glen Wesley with a high stick to the face and drew blood. There was only one referee in those days, and MacCreary missed it. Volatile Bruins Coach Terry O'Reilly was incensed and held up the game for over five minutes while making pleas and hurling insults at a seemingly unfazed MacCreary. Finally, when order appeared restored and the puck was about to be dropped, a fan decided to administer justice. He jumped over the end boards and ran at the referee. Unfortunately for the fan, the biggest linesman in the NHL happened to be working that game. Ron "Bear" Asselstine saw what was coming and charged from the blue line. He slammed into the fan who flew headlong into the end boards as the crowd roared. What a hit! Aaron Donald on skates!

Don't Know What You've Got 'Til It's Gone

THE VALUE AND QUALITY of NHL officiating was never more apparent than in November of '93 when they went on strike for better wages. Replacement officials were called from minor pro and junior leagues, and the games were a mess. The replacements were reluctant to call penalties; it was rugby on skates. The NHL further complicated things by forcing the replacements to wear earphones and take instructions from supervisors in the stands. How, as a referee, can you explain a penalty that was only seen through another man's eyes?

Hear No Evil, See No Evil

JIM KYTE WAS A defenceman with the Winnipeg Jets in the '80s. He was big, he was strong, and he could fight. He also played with a handicap; he was legally deaf. When he went into a corner to fetch the puck he couldn't hear if anyone was behind him so he made use of the glass to catch their reflection. He used to joke that being hearing impaired was an advantage. When a coach would go into a rant, he'd just turn off his hearing aids.

The degree of his handicap was apparent late one night on a bus ride from Hartford to Boston. Among the crowd every night in Hartford were two blondes of the female variety. They would sit near ice level in revealing clothing and do whatever they could to distract the players. Each had the attributes to meet the challenge.

After the game one night, the Jets got on the bus to go to Boston. About ten minutes outside of Hartford, a commotion started. Traveling alongside the bus in the passing lane were the two ladies. They had their dome light on and were performing a strip show for the boys. The one on the passenger side used the open window to great advantage, north and south.

Everybody on the bus, players and coaches, executives and media, was on the one side straining to catch the show amidst the clamor of cat calls, wolf whistles, and laughter.

Everyone that is, but one. Jim Kyte was on the other side of the bus reading a book, oblivious to the goings on. He had his hearing aids out.

Walk a Mile in My Shoes

WHEN I HEAR OF players belittling another NHL city, I can't help but think back to Mario Marois. The veteran defenceman was traded by his home town Quebec Nordiques to the Winnipeg Jets in 1985. He arrived in a "sour" state of mind, he hated the move, and it was reflected in his play that first year. But over the next three seasons his misery turned to joy. His regard for Winnipeg took a total about-face.

The joy lasted until late in 1988 when he was devastated to learn he had been traded again. Where to? Back home, back to the Quebec Nordiques.

No Sweat

MARIO MAROIS HAD A dubious distinction: he didn't sweat during a game. After a game, his equipment was "bone-dry." Sometime later, however, his ventilation system would kick in, and Mario would be soaking wet. This usually happened on the postgame bus ride to the hotel. It would be 20 below, and Mario would holler from the back of the bus to have the air conditioning turned on. The driver would comply, and we'd all shudder.

Message Received Loud and Clear

IT TAKES RESOLVE FOR a coach to scratch a key veteran from the line-up. Often the veteran will pout and occasionally go as far as to demand a trade. Others respond in the affirmative.

In February '93, Coach John Paddock scratched Jet Thomas Steen for inferior play. In the two games immediately after, Steen scored four goals and five assists. He went on to be NHL player of the week with thirteen points in four games. Coach and player were vindicated.

Steen Hits for the Cycle

HOW OFTEN HAVE YOU seen a player score a goal and then be told moments later that his wife had given birth earlier in the day? Thomas Steen carried that to new heights.

Steen scored a goal in the first game after wife Mona had given birth to each of their four children, and each time, the goal was scored in the first period.

Howe about That

THE DAY TIE DOMI of the Jets became a father for the first time, he achieved the Gordie Howe hat trick. He scored a goal in the first period, won a fight in the second period, and gained an assist in the third.

(Both Domi and Steen had sons who went on to play in the NHL.)

All Business and No Play Make Jack a Dull Boy

IN 1980, I WAS talking with a Winnipeg Jet, and the subject of salary came up. He told me that his annual stipend was $55,000. I recall being envious. Less than fifteen years later, Keith Tkachuk's salary was more than one hundred times that amount. The change in salary structure brought with it a change in the players' approach to the game; it became more businesslike. In the early days, it was common to see the whole team gather at a night spot after the game; red eyes and headaches were prevalent at practice the next morning. The big money and the European influx changed a lot of that. Where there may have been fifteen or more players in party mode in the '80s, there were only four or five "good ol' boys" in the '90s. Many of the players (particularly eastern Europeans) would simply order room service and a glass of wine and call it a night. In the morning, the old guard would take an aspirin and "skate it off." By that time the newer players had called their agents, gone to the gym, and seen the massage therapist.

From a distance, I always thought the older approach had value. Teams seemed to bond more in those days; there seemed less jealousy. As well, you didn't have to imbibe to be part of the group. Laurie Boschman for one, never touched a drop and never missed a get-together.

Study in Contrast

LAURIE BOSCHMAN'S STYLE OF play and his lifestyle were opposite ends of the spectrum. He is a religious man who is currently involved in "Christian Ministries." He was also a penalty minutes leader. He is one of only sixteen players to collect 2,000 penalty minutes and 500 points.

Off the ice he was kind and considerate, but on the ice, he was ruthless. He was also a master in the faceoff circle.

One day he volunteered to teach my son Luke how to take a faceoff. Luke was eight years old and excited. He learned a lot that day and couldn't wait for his next game to try it out. However, after taking just two faceoffs with the "Boschman" approach, Luke was told he was too aggressive and wouldn't be allowed to take any more faceoffs. Nobody enjoyed that story more than Boschman.

From Billy Mosienko to Janet Gretzky

CONTRARY TO POPULAR BELIEF, not all records are meant to be broken. No NHL player will ever better the mark of Winnipeg's Billy Mosienko, who scored three goals in twenty-one seconds for the Chicago Black Hawks. Nobody will ever score two goals in less than four seconds. It's been done twice, once in 1931 by "Old Poison" Nels Stewart, and once in the mid-'90s by Jet defenceman Deron Quint.

With the abolition of tie games, the Jets' thirty-game winless streak may haunt the record books forever.

Others on the "tough to top" list:

Jet Dale Hawerchuk is the youngest player ever to collect five points in a game; he was eighteen. On another occasion, Hawerchuk became the only player in the modern era to collect five assists in one period. Dave Christian scored for the Jets seven seconds into his first NHL shift. Doug Smail is one of only four players to score five seconds into a game; the others are Bryan Trottier, Alexander Mogilny, and Merlyn Phillips. It'll be a while, but somebody will eventually challenge the record of Jet Teemu Selanne, who scored seventy-six goals as a rookie.

Getting away from the Jets, another mark that will never be topped belongs to Patrick Roy. The last time the Montreal Canadiens won the Stanley Cup, they went to overtime ten times. Roy and the Canadiens won all ten games.

I should also mention the "Janet Gretzky" record established by Phoenix Coyotes goaltender Brian Boucher. It started on New Years Eve 2004. Boucher was in goal when the Coyotes shut out the Los Angeles Kings. Janet Gretzky learned through her husband Wayne that the Coyotes had planned to play Sean Burke in net for the next game. She asked, "Why would you change goalies when Boucher was perfect last night?" Wayne (in his capacity as a team owner) agreed and advanced her argument to Coach Bobby Francis. Francis reconsidered, and Boucher went on to collect an NHL record five straight shut outs.

Prior to Boucher's streak of invincibility, Sean Burke had been number one for the best of reasons. The Coyotes were a cumulative plus thirty-seven when he started in goal, and minus twenty-four when he didn't.

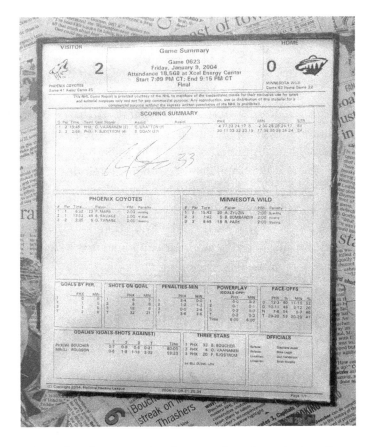

One of my few souvenirs: the game sheet from shut out five,
autographed post game by Brian Boucher.

Could Have Looked the Other Way

GAME FOUR OF BOUCHER'S five game streak was in Washington. Late in that game, the Coyotes found themselves vastly outnumbered. They had taken back-to-back penalties, and the Capitals pulled their netminder. It was six on three. Boucher and the penalty killers rose to the occasion, and the Coyotes prevailed 3–0. After the game, the referee went to Coach Bobby Francis and apologized for calling the second penalty. He explained that he hadn't realized a record was in the offing.

From Sunshine to Monsoon

WHEN YOU GAIN FIVE straight shutouts, you gain a lot of respect because obviously, the team is pretty good, right? No. The Coyotes won only two of their last twenty-two games that year. They missed the playoffs, and Coach Bobby Francis lost his job.

One Step Forward, One Step Back

THE WINNIPEG JETS/PHOENIX COYOTES constantly defied the theory of progressions. When things looked bad, they'd have a good season; when things looked good, they'd plummet. There are by-products to this type of behaviour.

The Jets had three "Coach of the Year" finalists in their seventeen seasons. Tom Watt and Bob Murdoch collected Jack Adams trophies, while in 1985, Barry Long was runner up to Mike Keenan in Philadelphia. All three were fired less than two full seasons later. A trend that continued when the franchise moved to Arizona and Bobby Francis went from toast to toasted.

Joe Btfstlk on Skates

JOE WHO? JOE WAS a character in the old Li'l Abner cartoons who always had a dark cloud over his head. Nothing ever went right for old Joe. I remember thinking of him in April of '96. It was the final regular season game for the original Jets, and it had immense implications. It was in Anaheim where the Mighty Ducks had fallen short and were merely closing out the season. For the Jets meanwhile, a win would vault them to a fourth-place finish and home ice in a playoff series against the Toronto Maple

Leafs. A loss on the other hand, would mean eighth place, and a date with the Detroit Red Wings, who had just established an NHL record by winning sixty-two games.

The Jets got "Joe Btfstlked" 5–2 in Anaheim.

The Jets did manage to win two playoff games against that Red Wing powerhouse, including game five in Detroit when they were outshot 52 to 19 and won 3–1. It was Nikolai Khabibulin's finest hour as a Jet.

Go Figure

IT WAS OFTEN SAID back in the day that Wayne Gretzky was no good on breakaways. I didn't agree with that because of what I had seen in the 1983 playoffs. It was game one of the Edmonton Oilers first round series with the Jets. Gretzky scored two shorthanded goals, plus one on the power play and one at even strength. The common factor: all were on breakaways; he went four for four.

That brings to mind the 1998 Winter Olympics in Nagano, Japan. You may recall the shoot-out between Canada and the Czech Republic. Each team selected five shooters. Wayne Gretzky, the greatest scorer the game has ever seen was not among Canada's five; it made no sense.

So why was it? Was it really Coach Marc Crawford's decision to ignore his most lethal weapon? The "Great One" sat and watched as Theo Fleury, Joe Niewendyk, Brendan Shanahan, Eric Lindros, and defenceman Ray Bourque were all denied by the great Dominik Hasek.

Years later, I asked Gretzky about that on two separate occasions. Both times he quickly changed the subject. "Curiouser and curiouser," because in a social setting Gretzky enjoys reminiscing about his hockey exploits, yet this was a topic to be avoided. We may never know the whole story.

In later years, Gretzky was quoted as saying had the shoot out gone to a sixth round, he would have been the man. That makes even less sense.

Victimized and Vilified

IT'S TRULY AMAZING HOW seemingly normal people can become so wrapped up in sports that they lose civility. Swedish people have a reputation of being placid and very easy to get along with. Tommy Salo may beg to differ.

The Swedish goaltender is not remembered for winning gold at the '94 Olympics near as much as he's remembered for a blown save eight years later in an Olympic quarter-final against Belarus. He was treated with disdain by many of his countrymen and never got over it.

One missed shot can have a profound impact on a legacy.

In Need of a Hat

THE FIRST TIME THE Phoenix Coyotes went to Pittsburgh, history was in the offing. Mario Lemieux needed three goals that night to tie Wayne Gretzky for the fastest to score 600 in a career. In the first period, Lemieux scored twice. By the third, he still needed one. Lemieux brought the crowd to their feet with two late breakaways. The first was stymied by an outstanding play by Coyote defenceman Teppo Numminen, and the second was ripped from him by goaltender Nikolai Khabibulin. Through 718 career games, Lemieux had 599 goals, Gretzky had 600.

Not Going to Take It Anymore

EVEN THE "MAGNIFICENT" AND the "Great" had their frustrating moments. One night, Mario Lemieux had had enough of Jet Peter Taglianetti's chirping and fired the puck at him; the thing was, Taglianetti was on the bench at the time. Another time Wayne Gretzky was driven to distraction by Jet Phil (Psycho) Sykes. He wanted Sykes penalized but to no avail. Gretzky reacted by firing the puck at the referee during a stoppage, but fortunately for Gretzky, Willie Lindstrom happened to be cruising by, and the puck hit his leg. People were left to wonder what would have happened had the "Great One" struck his target.

Heat-Seeking Missile

FORMER JET/COYOTE, DALLAS DRAKE had a different kind of game prep that would bring the building to life early. On his first shift, he would choose his prey, approach at speed, leave his feet and plaster his victim into the boards. Game on. It was blatant charging but was seldom called because of his relatively small size.

If Drake had been built like Eric Lindros, there'd still be repercussions.

Unrealistic Expectations

SOME HOCKEY PLAYERS RECEIVED less than a fair shake in Winnipeg. Three come to mind immediately:

Jimmy Mann was the Jets first pick in their first season. He had been an eighty-point man in the Quebec Junior league, but his real claim to fame is that he was "the toughest son of a bitch in the valley." At twenty years old, he challenged all comers and more than held his own. His hockey ability meanwhile, was a work in progress; he just wasn't ready. Fans and management wanted more than he could deliver. It's the curse of first- rounders who go to desperate teams. The ones with great skill, like Dale Hawerchuk can exceed expectations; the vast majority fall far short.

It always amazed me how some of the roughest, toughest, dirtiest players could also be the kindest people in the world off the ice. Jimmy's work with disabled people would have made him a candidate for NHL Humanitarian of the Year had the award been around then.

Andrew McBain also suffered the first-rounder curse. He was picked eighth overall by the Jets. He began his NHL career at eighteen, at least two years before he was ready. He had NHL talent, speed, skating ability, and a great shot; he just lacked seasoning and physical maturity. McBain, like Mann, was a likeable sort, always smiling. When a joke began to circulate that McBain played because he was John Ferguson's illegitimate son, he laughed and played along. It was a testament to his disposition.

Then there was Ray Neufeld, a victim if there ever was one. Neufeld was equipped to be a second liner on a poor team, a third liner on a good one. He was traded for a "top two" defenceman, Dave Babych. For some time after, Jets fans looked at Neufeld and thought Babych. It was totally out of his control. The Winkler, Manitoba native, had come home to a rude reception.

International Greats

THE JETS OF THE WHA put Winnipeg on the hockey map. They were league finalists five of the seven years and won the AVCO Cup three times. They traveled extensively to the Izvestia Cup tournament in Moscow, also to Sweden and Finland. They even played a game in Japan on a frozen swimming pool with a diving board at one end. In January of 1978, they became the first club team to ever beat the Soviet National team.

The WHA Jets were largely responsible for the infusion of Europeans in North American professional hockey. It was a controversial concept at the beginning. Veteran North American pros didn't like having to compete for jobs with interlopers. That feeling lasted until they began to realize how talented the likes of Anders Hedberg, Ulf Nilsson, Kent Nilsson, and Lars Eric Sjoberg were. The WHA Jets were the first true "internationals," and they revolutionized the game. Dump and chase was out; puck possession was in. Staying on your wing as if on a railroad track was replaced by freelancing. The line of Bobby Hull, Anders Hedberg, and Ulf Nilsson was one of the greatest of all time.

In 1976, the WHA Jets challenged the Montreal Canadiens to a showdown series. The challenge was rejected because the Canadiens had everything to lose and nothing to gain. That was the great Montreal team that finished with sixty wins and only eight losses en route to the Stanley Cup. For their part, the '76 Jets believe to a man they would have given the Canadiens all they could handle. Bobby Hull felt the Jets were equal to the Canadiens on the forward lines and in goal (Joe Daley with Winnipeg, Ken Dryden with Montreal) but inferior to the Canadiens on the blue line. That Montreal defence included Serge Savard, Larry Robinson, and Guy Lapointe.

How to Impress the Coach

ONCE AT THE IZVESTIA Cup tournament in Moscow, Jet defenceman Barry Long found himself the lone man back on a rush by Helmuts Balderis of the Soviet Nationals. Long decided to nail the speedy Soviet with a hip check on open ice. It didn't faze Balderis, who simply leaped over the defenceman and, without missing a beat, picked up the puck on the other side and went in to score. The goal was such a work of art that Jet defenceman Thommie Bergman instinctively stood up on the Jet bench and cheered! Bergman was stapled to the bench for the rest of the period.

Capitalist Perk

WHEN PLAYERS FROM IRON Curtain countries began arriving to play professionally in North America, one of the things they had to be taught was how to grocery shop. They would get to the meat counter with their eyes as big as saucers and instinctively begin to gather large amounts. They had to be convinced that, unlike back home, there would be an ample supply of goods at the store again the next day.

(Much like TP in North America in 2020)

Whatever You Say Sir

BY BRINGING THE NHL back to Winnipeg, Marc Chipman became the city's most popular and most prominent citizen. He could do no wrong. So, when he tried to ignore the overwhelming demand to rename the team the "Jets," people let him off the hook. He could call them the "Roughriders" and dress them in green and white polka dots as long as he brought them to Winnipeg.

The reluctance to name the team carried right into June. The NHL draft was quickly approaching, and the team had to have a name by then to avoid being a laughingstock. Thus, it made for great television when Chipman took the stage for the announcement. Tens of thousands were hoping the old name with all its memories would be reinstated. What would the new boss do? Well, seldom do people who share the same dream react so differently. While Chipman looked down and nearly choked when he murmured "Jets," thousands of his adoring fans cheered wildly. Another glorious chapter had been added to their celebration. Who says a name is just a name?

Bye-Bye Bee

ONE OF FRIAR'S WHA stories was about Kim Clackson and the Stinger Bee. Clackson wasn't all that big (5'10 195lbs) but was one the toughest hombres the game has ever seen. He was a graduate of the Paddy Ginnell school of intimidation (the junior Bombers) in Flin Flon. He could become unglued.

The Cincinnati WHA team was known as the "Stingers." Prior to each game, they'd turn the lights down in the rink and focus a spotlight on their mascot, a giant Bumble Bee that would circle the ice and stir up the crowd. Clackson could hear the "buzz" from the Jets' dressing room and, out of the blue, sprung up and hollered, "I'm going to get me a Stinger Bee!" He then charged out into the darkness and flew into the spotlight, where he decked the unsuspecting Bumble Bee.

Bedlam ensued. It was the Bee's last bumble.

The Flin Flon Bombers junior team set the framework for the "Broad Street Bullies" of Philadelphia. They played the same ultra-aggressive physical style. Bobby Clarke and

Reggie Leach went from Flin Flon to Philadelphia. They went from being coached by Paddy Ginnell to being coached by Fred Shero. Shero's mantra was, "Take the shortest route to the puck carrier, and arrive in ill humour."

Trivia: Shero, Ginnell, Clarke, and Leach are all Manitobans by birth.

It Was All or Nothing

IN 1996, WHEN THE Jets pulled the plug on Winnipeg and headed south, I was out of work. What to do? I was forty-seven years old and had nothing on my plate. I was sure I could work radio or television news in Winnipeg, but that's not what I wanted. I'd been spoiled by spending my time talking hockey and watching great athletes perform night after night. There was only one answer: follow the team to Phoenix.

Almost immediately, I caught a flight south. All the while I was on the plane, I envisioned the interview process. I thought of answers to every conceivable question I could be asked on why I deserve to broadcast Coyote hockey. I was totally prepared.

The next morning in Phoenix, I went directly to the downtown office of the Coyotes. I saw a secretary and asked her if Team President Sean Hunter was in his office. She replied, "Yes, have you got an appointment?" I didn't answer. I barged by her and burst into the president's office. I immediately proclaimed: "There's only one person for the voice of the Phoenix Coyotes, and you're looking at him!" The startled president replied, "Who the hell are you?"

It was the first of several questions I'd rehearsed the answer to. He got up from his desk and headed toward the parking lot. He was running late for a flight. All the way down the elevator and right to his car, I was in his ear selling myself. As he drove off, I was still talking. Once he was out of sight, I paused and laughed. I remember thinking, *Even if I don't get the job, I'll know I gave it a hell of a shot.*

A week later, I got the call: the job was mine!

Where Do I Know You From?

WHEN THE JETS WENT to Phoenix, they weren't going to a virgin hockey market. Phoenix had previously been home to a very successful pro franchise. The Roadrunners had won a couple of championships in the Western Professional Hockey League and sometimes outdrew their NBA counterparts, the Phoenix Suns. Their building, the Arizona Veterans Memorial Coliseum, became known as the "Madhouse on McDowell."

The Coyotes, though, came with the NHL banner and attracted the curious. On any given night, as much as seventy percent of the crowd had never seen a hockey game before. For the most part, they enjoyed what they saw, going as far as to cheer "icing."

The team's first president, Sean Hunter, had a mandate to make the Coyotes #1 in the marketplace. They would be bigger than Jason Kidd, Steve Nash and the Suns, bigger than the struggling Cardinals of the NFL, and solidly positioned before the arrival of the expansion Arizona Diamondbacks. The players, the coaches, and the broadcasters were seen everywhere. People would pose for a picture with us then ask, "By the way, who are you?" We taught hockey classes at schools; we appeared at carnivals, barbeques, and golf tournaments. In late August, we would go on tour and speak to different organizations in rural Arizona. The Budweiser people were one hundred percent committed and played a part in every promotion. During a home stand, I'd often spend more time with them than the team. One night they had me doing play-by-play of a board-hockey game in a crowded bar. It was time-consuming but fun and well worth the effort. The banners were seen everywhere.

Like all new things, the novelty waned over time, and the promotional events dwindled. Then, in 2002, the bottom began to fall out. New President Doug Moss came in, and there were unexplained firings right and left. Then their replacements were fired. Continuity was lost, paranoia abounded. Sponsors no longer had a point of contact within the organization and took their business elsewhere. It was a costly, needless mess that undermined much of what we had built.

A Team of Many Factions

THERE WERE SOME GROWING pains for the Coyotes.

The first arena (then known as America West) was made for basketball. The sightlines for hockey rendered 3,000 upper deck seats basically useless; they only provided a view of two-thirds of the ice. In the beginning, those seats were snapped up by the college crowd because they went for $8 each, and there was a party atmosphere provided by a local rock station (KDKB). After a couple of years however, they couldn't give those seats away.

There was duplication in the front office. In the first year, the Coyotes had two general managers and that caused no end of confusion. Who do you approach if you want to make a deal, John Paddock or Bobby Smith? Paddock had been with the franchise in that capacity over the last years in Winnipeg. Bobby Smith was a Minnesota hockey icon who was hired by new Coyotes Owner Richard Burke (from Minnesota). As you might imagine, that didn't end well for Paddock.

There were two assistant general managers, Mike Ohearn, who'd come from Winnipeg, and Taylor Burke, the young son of the aforementioned owner. That wasn't a problem though, because Taylor was there more to learn than to do. He was also the eyes and ears of the new ownership.

The other office people had come from four different areas, and each had their own idea on how things should be handled. There were the people who'd come down from Winnipeg. There were some from Minnesota. The president, Sean Hunter, had brought people in from Denver, and there was a smattering of Phoenicians. An "Ununited" Nations of hockey ideas.

Less Stress Is Not for Everybody

DEPENDING ON YOUR PERSONALITY, playing hockey in Phoenix can be advantageous or detrimental. Away from the rink, players and coaches are seldom recognized; life is more peaceful. Some like it that way. Other players need recognition, albeit for different reasons. For every Jeremy Roenick, who lives for the adulation, there's another player equally motivated by fear of failure. A fear that is multiplied by the spotlight in hockey markets like Montreal and Winnipeg.

Newbies

THE FIRST YEAR IN Phoenix did bring about a couple of chuckles.

There was a reporter from a Phoenix newspaper who wrote that goalie Darcy Wakaluk hailed from the "heart of the Saskatchewan Rockies." The same reporter saw his first snow in Edmonton. When practice was cancelled that day because of a long flight from Montreal, he wrote it was cancelled due to the bitter cold. It was October 29th.

A lady who was a football and basketball fan was quite excited when presented with tickets to her first hockey game. The next day I asked how it went, and she replied, "It was great! We loved it!" There was one problem, however. She and her elderly mother decided to leave early to beat the rush. She was amazed that everyone else had the same idea. "They all left after the third quarter!" (Third period).

Over and Done

A PART OF THE job I considered most valuable was a pregame one-on-one talk with the head coach. It was an opportunity to establish a rapport and to get up-to-date information on who was and wasn't playing, and hopefully the reason why. Some coaches were more forthcoming than others.

One who was reserved and generally didn't open up any more than he absolutely had to was former Coyotes Coach Jim Schoenfeld. One night in Detroit, he told me he would be a little late for our chat and politely asked me to wait. After a while, the coach's door opened, and Mike Gartner stormed out. I entered to see Schoenfeld staring at the floor, misty eyed. I asked what the problem was? He looked me in the eye and asked, "Have you any idea how tough it is to tell a 700-goal scorer that he can't play anymore?"

It happened so fast. One year earlier, Gartner led the franchise out of the gate with a league-leading ten goals in ten games. He scored the first- ever Coyote goal, scored their first hat trick, and in his 1300th game, he scored the Coyotes' first shorthanded goal.

Fifteen months later, it was determined he couldn't play.

Shot from the Gate in '98!

AT THE END OF November '98, the Phoenix Coyotes were riding a fourteen-game unbeaten streak and the best record in the NHL. They'd also achieved a couple of rare feats:

1. They had more points in the standings (thirty) than goals against (twenty-six).

2. They had gone seventeen consecutive games without allowing more than two goals, something no team had accomplished since the 1950s.

They were getting outstanding goaltending from both Nikolai Khabibulin and Jimmy Waite. They were strong on the blue line with Teppo Nummenin, Gerald Diduck, Keith Carney, and Jyrki Lumme. The forwards, including Keith Tkachuk and Jeremy Roenick, had bought in on the defensive system preached by Coach Jim Schoenfeld, at least for a while.

By mid-March, everything had changed. The Coyotes were in free fall with only two wins in thirteen games. General Manager Bobby Smith indicated that Schoenfeld's job was on the line if the team didn't win a March 13th home game against Anaheim. The "Bulin Wall" rose to the challenge. Nikolai Khabibulin shut out the Ducks 1–0. It led to a five-game unbeaten string, and Schoenfeld was spared until the season ended.

Opposite, but the Same

THE COYOTES WERE NUMBER one in the NHL at the end of November '98 due to their defense. At the end of November, the following year, they were again number one, but because of offense. Under new Coach Bobby Francis they had become the NHL's highest scoring team.

An Eye for an Eye

BY THE COYOTES' THIRD season, they had built an immense dislike for the Dallas Stars. To paraphrase Coyotes Assistant Coach John Tortorella: the Stars are so arrogant it's sickening. Every game between the teams was physical and cheap shots abounded. It came to a head in late March of '99. The Stars (Craig Ludwig in particular) were doing all they could to get under the skin of Jeremy Roenick. It didn't take long for Roenick to respond. It was still in the first period when he ran Mike Modano and put him out of the game. The thing was, Modano didn't have the puck at the time. Roenick was assessed a major penalty, and because he also got a game misconduct, the Stars would have to wait to exact revenge.

Now normally, when there's a whole lot of talk about retribution, nothing much happens, but it did this time. 6'5" Stars Captain Derian Hatcher announced to the world that Roenick would pay. The league warned of consequences, but Hatcher paid no heed. In the first period of the next game in Dallas, Hatcher charged Roenick and plastered him into the boards. Roenick's jaw was broken in three places.

Hatcher was suspended for seven games, including the first five of the playoffs. The Stars, however, overcame his absence and went on to win the Stanley Cup.

(The Coyotes and Stars didn't meet again for seven months, but the bitterness remained. In their first meeting the next season, Coyote Keith Tkachuk called out Hatcher before the game was two minutes old. The two captains went at it right at centre ice, and while Tkachuk didn't win the battle, he did earn an immense degree of respect from his teammates and coaches.

In later years, Roenick wrote in his book (J.R.) that he never played with a captain who took greater care of his people than Keith Tkachuk did.)

Observations and Questions

IN NOV 2001, THERE was champagne in the Coyotes' dressing room. The occasion was the first NHL goal for Radoslav Suchy. It came in his 162nd game. He scored late in the third period when the Coyotes had a two-man advantage and a 5–1 lead.

Fans and teammates love it when the tough guy has a big offensive night. Louis Debrusk scored two for the Coyotes in a playoff game against St. Louis, and Jim Mackenzie notched a hat trick at home.

I've always wondered how many toes and feet Al MacInnes broke over his illustrious career. His one hundred-mile-per-hour point blasts were only two or three inches off the ice. I know Teppo Numminen was victimized often. There were many others. To his credit, MacInnes was known to hold off on a shot if a player's face was particularly vulnerable.

When Nikolai Khabibulin turned down a three-year, 9-million-dollar contract offer from the Coyotes, General Manager Bobby Smith said he wouldn't be surprised if Khabibulin sat the whole season. As it turned out, he did and most of the following year as well before signing with Tampa Bay. And while he did win a Stanley Cup in Tampa, it wasn't a bad thing for the Coyotes. By losing Khabibulin, they gained Sean Burke, who signed for the exact contract Khabibulin passed on, and Burke performed brilliantly.

In November of 2002, a Coyotes player got hold of some invisible ink, and suddenly everything was bathed in purple. It was all over the player's hands and their equipment and the dressing room walls were a mess. Nobody knew who was responsible. Every player was affected except one. For some strange reason, the purple haze didn't find its way to defenceman Todd Simpson.

Portland Coyotes

THE ARIZONA COYOTES HAVE undergone a number of ownership changes, but the most celebrated was one that involved Wayne Gretzky. It was a change that very nearly didn't happen.

Steve Ellman who headed the second ownership group, was in financial trouble. He reached out to Gretzky to become a minority partner. He believed the Gretzky name would increase the value of the team, and new investors would take an interest. Gretzky repeatedly said "no," but Ellman persisted. Ellman's pleading carried into the eleventh hour of a deadline when Gretzky finally relented. Had Gretzky not agreed, the Coyotes would have moved to Portland, Oregon. They had a standing offer to move there from the late Paul Allen, who was reportedly the second richest man in the US at that time (after Bill Gates).

It's Good When Your Ball Drops

EXCESSIVE GREED AND STUBBORNNESS cost the NHL the entire 2004–2005 season. As a result, the draft order the following June had to be established by using more than the usual number of ping pong balls. The Pittsburgh Penguins ball was the last one to drop, and they had themselves a generational player, Sidney Crosby.

I recall when it got down to the final two teams. Crosby would go to either Pittsburgh or Anaheim. I had a disagreement with a cohort of mine who also worked for the Phoenix Coyotes. Whose side would you have taken? Darren Pang hoped Pittsburgh would win the lottery so the Coyotes would not have to face Crosby as often. I wanted Anaheim's ball to drop so we could see him a lot.

The formula in those days was to have each eastern team meet each western team twice over a three-year period. Meanwhile, you saw clubs in your own division eight times a season. Thus, in three years, the Coyotes would see the Penguins twice; they'd see the Ducks twenty-four times.

You can never get the great ones in your building often enough.

Is Tonight a Two or a Three?

I'VE NEVER UNDERSTOOD THE logic in having some games worth two points and others worth three. It invites the type of scenario that happened on April 5th, 2001.

It was the final weekend of the season, and it was nail-biting time. In the west, only two points separated the fifth- place team from the ninth. One of the five teams would be eliminated. The Coyotes played their final two games on the road in San Jose and Anaheim. The Saturday game in San Jose was played early, and the Sharks prevailed. However, the Coyotes were still a breathing entity. A win the next afternoon in Anaheim against the last place Ducks would, in all likelihood, secure a playoff spot. The only scenario that could render their final game meaningless was if the Vancouver Canucks prevailed in a three-point game later that Saturday night.

The Coyotes got off the plane in Anaheim to learn that Murphy's Law had been served. The Vancouver Canucks defeated the Los Angeles Kings in overtime. The two points awarded the Canucks, and the single point gained by the Kings, were exactly enough to eliminate the Coyotes.

If You've Seen One Steen, You've Seen 'Em All

BACK WHEN THE COYOTES played in a major league facility in Glendale, they had what they called the "Ring of Honor" high above the ice surface. It paid tribute to great players who'd been with the franchise since its inception in Winnipeg. There was #9 Bobby Hull, #10 Dale Hawerchuk, #27 Teppo Numminen, and #25 Thomas Steen. There was also one "retired" Coyotes jersey, #19 Shane Doan.

On Steen's night, he and I and Team Executive Cliff Fletcher were at centre ice for the ceremony. Fletcher had in his hands a covered painting that we assumed to be of Thomas Steen in his Jets jersey. Near the end of the ceremony, with great fanfare, Thomas unwrapped the picture and looked at it awkwardly. The picture was a collage of Thomas' achievements with a face in the centre. The face of "Anders" Steen. Anders Steen had a forty-two-game career as a Jet; he scored five goals.

Thomas Steen is generally pretty quiet, but when I saw him two weeks later in Minnesota, he hollered from the far side of the press box, "Hey Curt, what am I going to do with this giant picture of Anders?" And then we laughed.

Did You See Anything?
I Didn't See Anything

ONLY IN A PLACE like Phoenix could a faux pas like the Steen picture go virtually unnoticed. I was expecting Canadian sports networks to be all over it the next day. But nobody knew about it, not one phone call. There were repercussions within the organization. Wayne Gretzky and General Manager Mike Barnett, who watched the ceremony from the press box, were livid and demanded answers, but everything was kept in-house.

Oh, and the giant picture? It was redone, and the central figure now bears a striking resemblance to "Thomas" Steen.

Isn't There a Toronto Team?

SOMETIMES A TEAM'S RECORD against another can be skewed for reasons that aren't readily apparent. Over five seasons between 1998 and 2003, the Phoenix Coyotes were zero for five against the Toronto Maple Leafs. The thing is, the Coyotes were the road team every time. The Leafs did not play a single game in Phoenix for five years.

The Leafs were a huge draw in western Canada and would play an extra road game or two there. In trade, the Coyotes would get an extra visit from the likes of the New York Rangers or Boston Bruins. The NHL never publicizes that kind of arrangement.

The Aborted Comeback?

I CAN'T RECALL THE year offhand, but 2003 would be close. I got a call while on summer vacation. Al Strachan of *The Globe and Mail* asked if I knew anything about Wayne Gretzky making an NHL comeback with the Phoenix Coyotes? I said, "No, I'm sure there's nothing to it." I regret that I did nothing. I should have checked it out, but the idea seemed so far-fetched that I didn't. I was irresponsible.

A few days later, I arrived in Phoenix in time for training camp and there he was, "The Great One," skating every drill, working every rush. He was the first player on the ice and the last to leave. I was told that he had previously attended the rookie camp and never missed an on-ice session.

Was it true then? Would the number 99 again be seen on NHL ice? He certainly wasn't saying. It all led to the Coyotes annual inter-squad game at their practice facility in Scottsdale. The place was packed. Everyone had to see for themselves.

However, the dream died that night; the magic was gone. Gretzky wasn't a shadow of his former self. When training camp resumed the next morning, there was no Gretzky.

Double Up

IN THE EARLY DAYS, teams would travel to the rink or airport on one bus. The coach had one assistant. There were two radio guys and one from each of the two newspapers.

In recent years teams have needed two buses. Room had to be made for the goaltending coach and two or three more assistants, including a massage therapist. There are also television people.

In Phoenix, the entourage would include the group known as FOG (friends of Gretzky). This would include his business manager/ travel secretary and his tennis pro.

Where Is Everybody?

PRIOR TO A FIVE-GAME road trip in December of '06, Coach Wayne Gretzky said he thought his Coyotes could sweep the trip. It was a bold statement for a couple of reasons. One, the Coyotes were five games below 500 at the time, and the other is the fact that no NHL team had swept a five-game road trip in over four years. Lo and behold, they did it, including a game in Atlanta where they overcame a 4–1 third period deficit.

So now suddenly, there was reason for optimism. The Coyotes were a 500 team and only five points out of a playoff spot with half the season left. They were going home to play the Detroit Red Wings. I recall looking forward to that game, not only because the Red Wings were good and the Coyotes were hot, but also because the Red Wings always drew a raucous crowd in Phoenix. I expected a sell out.

Instead, they had one of the worst crowds of the year, and they deserved it. The Coyotes organization doubled the ticket prices for that game. Thousands of Red Wing fans who only attended when Detroit was in town, refused to pay the ransom.

A month or so later, the Red Wings would return for their second and final visit. Two weeks prior to that game, the Coyotes announced a two-for-one ticket sale on the Red Wings game only. It didn't matter; the damage was done. Many Red Wings fans vowed to never return.

As it turned out, the Detroit fans missed Pavel Datsyuk at his finest. In winning both games in Phoenix, the Red Wings scored a total of nine goals. Pavel Datsyuk had nine points.

It's common practice for NHL teams to alter ticket prices depending on who the visitors are but 100%? In Phoenix?

The Mouth of the Gift Horse

TO MY MIND, JETS President Barry Shenkarow never understood the value of television. He was convinced that if a game was televised, the fans would stay home. I think otherwise. I believe that constant exposure creates a buzz and a desire to get closer to the action. Television is a tease that can lure people to the rink. How often while watching a game on television have you heard someone say, "Man, I wish I was there!" A Teemu Selanne breakaway goal was fun to watch on TV, but at the rink, you not only saw it, you FELT it, along with thousands of others.

Thus, the Jets local television package was only sixteen games a season. They could have carried more, but Shenkarow would only allow eight home games to be televised. The TV stations (CKY and CKND) would offer to do an equal number of home and road, citing the fact they lost money televising road games.

What happened in Chicago illustrates the point. Owner Bill Wirtz was adamant that no home games would be televised. Under him in 2004, ESPN named the Chicago Black Hawks the worst franchise in pro sport. When he passed in 2007, his son took over and began televising at home. The Black Hawks' average attendance jumped immediately, from 13,000 to 17,000 and ultimately to 21,000.

Shenkarow had television at his disposal and chose to dispose of it.

Blowing Fuses

OFTEN IN HOCKEY, THE most reactionary people are the general managers. People like John Ferguson, Brian Burke, Lou Nanne, and Ron Caron.

Caron was the general manager in St. Louis. His private box was alongside our broadcast location with a glass partition between. If something went wrong, he would lash out at the visiting broadcasters only because we were right there. It was priceless. His bald head would break into a sweat, his face would go crimson and round, his eyes would bulge and glaze, and his flaring nose would flatten as he pushed it into the glass. All the while, he'd be screaming obscenities, waving his arms, and referring to the Jets as "your team!" One night the Jets scored a goal that should not have been allowed but was; it came just as time had expired in the first period. Predictably, Caron went ballistic. The thing was, as he was screaming at me through the glass, I kept remembering that he was to be my intermission guest. Could I put him on the air in his frenzied state?

Of course, I did. It was guaranteed to be great radio. I did, however, tell our operator that at the first sign of "language," he was to cut Caron's mic. Caron took a seat alongside me, still cussing and screaming until the very second the commercial ended. I said, "I understand you're a little upset about how the period ended?" His passionate reply was clean as a whistle. It was remarkable. After the interview, I congratulated him on his professionalism, at which time he went "bonkers" again.

A Trade Unlike Any Other

LOU NANNE WAS THE general manager of the Minnesota North Stars. One night in Winnipeg, Nanne was convinced his team had scored, but the goal light wasn't pushed on and play continued. The goal judge was the late Joe Walker. Two weeks later, the North Stars were back, and the same thing happened again at Joe Walker's end of the ice. Nanne, in a fit of pique, raged, "I'm making a trade...for that @#*%ing goal judge!"

Peter Nearly Died Young

THE JETS WERE CHARTERING home immediately after ANOTHER playoff loss in Edmonton when sportscaster Peter Young decided to go to the front of the plane and share a story with John Ferguson. Young mentioned that he had recently been at Wayne Gretzky's house for a barbecue and had a great time. It was NOT what Ferguson needed to hear at that moment. The Jets general manager hissed, then he growled, and then he exploded!

It was a scene right out of the comic books. Peter broke into a dead run toward the back of the plane hollering, "I'm sorry, John! I'm sorry!" Ferguson was hot on his heels, shaking his fist and barking expletives!

Calm was eventually restored, although Fergie continued to fume. Young, meanwhile, was left to ponder the realization that had it been possible to open a window, he could have received a whole different indoctrination into the 30,000-foot club.

Ballard Ballads

BACK WHEN HAROLD BALLARD owned and staffed Maple Leaf Gardens, I was always under the impression that ageism was practiced in the building. No one under the age of one hundred need apply for work.

Ballard was a character. He didn't care what people thought of him; he had his team, he had his building, he had lots of money, and he had his buddy, King Clancy.

In my rookie year, Friar asked me to tape an interview with Ballard. I recall being a little tentative, and I suppose it showed. I said, "Excuse me, Mr. Ballard, I'm with Winnipeg radio; can I get an interview with you?" He looked at me, laughed, and said, "First off, the name's Harold, and secondly, sit down and shoot the shit for a while." We had a great visit, and then he said, "Turn on the mic and ask me anything at all!" It was perfect coming only days after Daryl Sittler had ripped the "C" off his jersey. It was one of many interviews I wish I'd kept.

Fair is Foul and Foul is Fair

ALL THE WHILE WE did the Jets on CKY radio, CJOB radio did their own pre- and postgame shows. We, as the rights holders, did our pre- and post- from the rink; CJOB was relegated to restaurants in the area. It was competition, and the listener benefitted. Both stations went out of our way to outdo the other.

One time when the Leafs were coming, I called Harold Ballard and asked if he would come on our postgame show. He agreed, and we began promoting it immediately. However, CJOB pulled a quickie; they called Ballard to remind him that the postgame show was done at CHI-CHI's restaurant and not at the rink. They would have someone escort him. Word got out; I was livid. Ballard couldn't be two places at once. I then called in a favour. I asked John Ferguson to convince his old buddy Harold to do both shows but go to the rights holder first. So, Mr. Ballard showed up, and we just happened to do the longest post game show imaginable. By the time Ballard got to CHI-CHI's restaurant, it was last call.

As I said, I was initially upset at the subterfuge, but, in retrospect, it was a great move on their part. I believe current Saskatoon Blades broadcaster Les Lazaruk was the perpetrator.

Praise from on High

THE OLD CHECKERDOME IN St. Louis had a tiered press box. The visiting radio position was in the front row, right in the middle. Thus, everyone nearby, including those immediately behind, couldn't help but hear the visiting play-by-play. (Whether they wanted to or not.)

One night the first period had just ended when I got a tap on the shoulder. I looked back to see the smiling face of Gordie Howe. He told me he was listening to my commentary and enjoying it. I couldn't believe it, "Mr. Hockey" was complimenting me! It's something I'll never forget for a couple of reasons. One, considering the source, it's the greatest compliment I ever got. And two, the last two periods were the hardest ever to broadcast. It kept running through my mind: *Gordie's behind me, watching, listening, judging. I* couldn't concentrate the rest of the night.

How Did I Get Here?

ONE OF THE MOST accommodating people in hockey was Jacques Demers; he had time and a smile for everybody. One night when he was coaching in Detroit, I went to the hallway outside the Red Wings room and asked Jacques if I could tape an interview with him. He asked me to wait because he was about to have a pregame meeting with his team. Then before I could answer, he said, "Ah, what the heck, come and sit in on the meeting." It was the last place I expected to be, in the Red Wings dressing room, being a party to the coach's pregame speech.

It was enlightening but very simple. So, when he was done, I turned on the mic and said, "So that's it, stop Hawerchuk and stop Carlyle and you beat the Jets?" He laughed and elaborated. He went on to be "Coach of the Year" that season.

Talk to Me

DEALING WITH THE MEDIA is a daily occurrence for professional athletes. Some despise it, others embrace it. Two of the latter come to mind immediately.

One is Robert Picard, a defenceman who played for the Jets in the mid-eighties. Picard never saw a microphone he didn't like, and no question was off-limits. He was great to have at team functions because he enjoyed taking the stage to help with the entertainment.

The other is Eddy Olczyk, who not surprisingly became a hockey commentator and horse race analyst. I used to tape an interview with a Jet every game-day morning. Olczyk noticed this and wanted to be the man, but I kept going elsewhere. One day he just came right out and asked why I never interviewed him? I said, "Eddy, I'm saving you for a day when I don't feel well, because I know I won't have to talk much."

Two weeks later, in St. Louis, it happened. I said, "Eddy, I got the flu." He said, "Great!" I asked him two questions, and the intermission wasn't long enough.

Bedfellows?

I DON'T KNOW OF any journalist who supported the NHL Players Association to the degree that Al Strachan did. He was constantly at odds with the likes of Gary Bettman and Brian Burke. I had the impression that if the players were paid a billion dollars a year, Strachan would argue that they should get two billion. With that in mind, I asked a Players Association representative if Strachan was on the payroll? He laughed and said, "No, he's not, but he is the first person we call with breaking news." It was a win-win alliance.

No Name, No Go

HOCKEY BROADCASTING IS AN easy job, and it's a lot of fun. The toughest games to do are the ones with the smallest audiences: the exhibition games. You've got players you've never heard of suiting up on both sides and wearing obscure numbers.

I was always lucky at exhibition time. The various Jets and Coyotes equipment managers: Jack "Smokey" Stouffer, Craig "Zinger" Heisinger, and Stan Wilson would not allow a player to step on the ice without wearing his name, even if he was a last-minute arrival. It was a point of pride. Some other teams didn't care about that. I remember calling one NHL exhibition game in Brandon, Manitoba, when two players had the same number (63) and no name plates. Do you suppose they saw the writing on the wall?

The hardest working people in hockey and probably all professional sports are the equipment handlers. They're the first people at the rink in the morning and the last to leave. And the most amazing thing: they're always upbeat!

It's Nothing, Really

PEOPLE OFTEN ASK HOW a broadcaster can identify the players so quickly when there are forty players dressed for every game. Actually, if you work with one of the teams, it's very easy. You're going to know the twenty players you cover every day, which cuts the list in half. Then take the Edmonton Oilers as a glaring example. Every hockey fan of the day could readily identify Paul Coffey, Mark Messier, and Wayne Gretzky. They'd also be familiar with Kevin Lowe, Glen Anderson, Jari Kurri, Grant Fuhr, and Dave Semenko. Toss in standouts like Kent Nilsson or Ken Linseman, and many of the bases are covered. The Oilers were more easily recognized than most of course but, even lower profile teams like the Hartford Whalers and New Jersey Devils had some marquee players.

So, on any given night, there would be no more than a handful of players who might require a broadcaster to take a quick glance at a program.

If you're tuned to a hockey broadcast and hear the announcer say "Here come the Flyers out of their own zone" it's safe to assume he doesn't have a clue which Flyer has the puck.

Inflated Perspective

LOCAL HOCKEY BROADCASTERS ARE often accorded status beyond our worth. We're identified with the favourite team and by extension become the favourite broadcaster.

People who are now middle-aged have often told me how they would smuggle a small radio into their room after bedtime and listen quietly to the exploits of their team. My voice was the last they would hear before nodding off, and it created a bond.

It was the same everywhere in Western Canada. People in Vancouver thought Jim Robson was the best; hockey fans in Calgary lived and died with Peter Maher. In Edmonton, Rod Phillips was revered as the "voice" of one of the greatest hockey teams of all time. The local "radio guy" was there for every minute of every game, every success, and every failure.

Time and "progress" has changed that. With so many games being televised and so many different broadcast crews involved, a lot of the singular identity has been lost. Television doesn't have the intimacy of radio.

Who's that Guy?

A WINNIPEG RADIO STATION (CITI FM) had a sound-alike contest. People would call in and do an imitation of me: calling a goal, or a save, or any other moment of anxiety during a Jets game. Cousins Rick Loewen and James Loewen (The 2 Sports Guys) initiated it, and it went over well. In fact, the winner got to do his impersonation at the Arena, during a Jets game. I must say I was flattered, and I enjoyed it; I was also in for a surprise. I heard the show a few times and always laughed at what I felt were exaggerated imitations. I recall thinking, *I don't do that.* Then one day, I was editing tape of a Jets broadcast and suddenly, I heard it too. I exclaimed, "I do that! I'm doing exactly what the mimickers picked up on!"

It was a feel-good revelation. I wasn't vanilla.

Inflexibility Defeats the Purpose of Live Broadcasts

TELEVISION IS SOMETIMES TOO regimented. Radio is strictly adlib; what you see is what you say. One of the first TV games I ever did featured the Edmonton Oilers and Winnipeg Jets. At one stage Doug Smail had been injured and was crawling on hands and knees to the Jet bench. I was describing it, and all the while, the young producer was hollering in my ear: "Talk about Gretzky! Talk about Gretzky!" I looked at the monitor, and sure enough, the camera was on Gretzky, who was standing in the faceoff circle watching Smail. I finished my thought on Smail and was chastised for it after the game. Welcome to a new world.

I always found more experienced television producers good to work with, they're flexible, the broadcasts are collaborative efforts and everything flows. Many younger producers take a while to gain that confidence. In their anxiety to put their personal stamp on a production, they stick to a rigid format and the broadcast gets choppy.

Not the Cuckoo's Nest

ONE NIGHT IN LOS Angeles, we were doing a radio game between the Kings and the Phoenix Coyotes. Our host, Todd Walsh, found actor Jack Nicholson in the crowd and asked if he could have a few words with him. Nicholson's reply was, "I don't do radio." I relate this story because I've often been asked which I prefer, radio or television? Obviously, from an ego standpoint, television has the advantage. I can recall people saying to me, "Oh, you're only on radio." It was demeaning. Another television advantage is money; it generally pays better. There is often less work on television; the broadcasters are spoon-fed information and led through the broadcast by a producer. When the game ends (often within ten seconds,) the play-by-play crew can be done for the night. Many radio play-by-play people arrange and do their own interviews, and in many cases, are an integral part of the pre and postgame shows.

There is, however, one huge advantage to radio, and that is individuality. You talk of what you see, and if a story springs to mind, you can relate it immediately; it's folksy. I've always preferred a good story to a replay of an offside, so from a satisfaction standpoint, I prefer radio.

Less Prattle

WHEN YOU'RE BROADCASTING A sport, the game is the thing; everything else should take a back seat. I've not found anyone (other than the odd TV producer) who enjoys listening to an interview while the game is going on. It defeats the purpose of sports telecasting. Interviews are what intermissions are for, particularly when you have two of them.

Once in Phoenix, a TV producer decided to have Coyotes General Manager Mike Barnett come on live during all three periods of a home game. We covered most everything in the first visit, so by the second period we were reaching, and the fact the Coyotes were down 4–0 didn't help. Fortunately, the rookie in control canceled the third period arrangement with the Coyotes down 6–0.

Psst...I'm over Here

HOW DO YOU FEEL when you're talking with someone and out of the blue, they begin to gaze out the window? Television does the equivalent all the time.

Watch the play-by-play person during an "on camera" segment. He will often look and sometimes even stare at the camera while his analyst is talking. It's not natural; it's just distracting, but is still taught at some broadcast schools. A notable exception to that habit is Jim Nantz, who maintains visual contact with his analyst. By doing so, Nantz creates the impression that he's interested in what his partner is saying.

The eye to the camera theory evolved in the early days of television as a means to have viewers feel included in the conversation. Its "best- before" date has long since passed.

Caught with Our Pants Down!

HAVE YOU EVER NOTICED how quickly the sports networks leave the rink to get back to the anchor desk? They do it in the hope you don't have time to change channels, and you'll get hooked on what you see afterward.

In Phoenix, a lot of our games were carried on FOX Sports Arizona. The very moment the game ended the producer would begin the countdown. I had eight seconds to sign off and introduce the FOX Sportsdesk. One night the game went to overtime, and the Coyotes scored. We signed off in eight seconds, then learned there had been a crease violation, and the goal was disallowed. Whoops. I'm amazed it hasn't happened more often.

Out with the New and in with the Old

HOCKEY PLAY-BY-PLAY ON TELEVISION has pretty much come full circle. In the early days when *Hockey Night in Canada* stood alone, broadcasters Foster Hewitt in Toronto and Danny Gallivan in Montreal did much the same style of play-by-play on television as they did on radio. Identify the location of the puck, name the player in possession of it, and portray the urgency of the situation.

Then when television became a bigger part of hockey, some play-by-play broadcasters pulled back a little, leaving the picture to tell much of the story. That approach picked up steam when the Americans got into it, and play-by-play became more "conversational." It's something that can be attributed to background. American broadcasters had a history in baseball and football, where there's a lot of time to converse between every pitch or every down. Hockey, on the other hand, demands constant attention. In the last few years, television play-by-play has reverted closer to its original form, and in the process brought much of the excitement back.

Nobody epitomized the change in the American approach more than Mike Emrick. When he began working hockey on television, he treated it like a science class; too much information and not enough excitement. Then one day, I heard him do a New Jersey Devils game on radio and thought, Wow, this guy's good! Why doesn't he broadcast that way on television? *The "Doc," as he's known, must have come to the same realization. He added his radio enthusiasm to his television delivery, spiced it with humour, and became one of the best in the business.*

Most NHL games are exciting, but there are some duds. When those come along, the broadcasters should rise to the challenge. There's no need to fib about what's going on, but you can add a little zip. It is, after all, entertainment.

I'm Doing What, Tonight?

OFTEN THE PRODUCTION LEVEL of a hockey telecast in Canada is superior to what you see originating in the US. There's a reason for that.

In Canada, hockey (particularly the NHL) is number one. The stations assign their best people to the production crew of the local hockey game. In the US, hockey often takes a back seat. If there happens to be an NFL, NBA, MLB, or even a college game in the same market on the same night, hockey can be relegated to secondary, even tertiary status or worse. The least experienced crew draws the assignment. To make matters worse, they may be unfamiliar with the game.

Sometimes it goes beyond television. In the Coyotes' first year, the beat reporter assigned to Coyotes coverage by a Phoenix newspaper confessed to having never seen a hockey game before in his life. It's akin to assigning the average North American reporter to cover Cricket.

Mumblings and Grumblings of an Old Man

I FIND IT FUNNY that so many play-by-play broadcasters have reverted to "grandmother" language. When I hear: "Goodness gracious me!", "My word!", or the ubiquitous, "My goodness!" my nanna springs to mind; she said all those things! Although thinking back, even the "man's man" didn't always walk the walk. In his last few years, broadcaster Harry Neale often spoke of a "lovely" pass. Nanna would have jitterbugged hearing that.

And another thing: Why do so many broadcasters get hung up on statistics? Tell me a story, set the scene, explain the consequence of the game, tell me what's going on in other games, but don't excite me with: "Nine points in sixteen games betters by one his mark of March 2015." Or, "This is game 157 of Joe's NHL career!" (Even Joe doesn't know that, so why should I care?) How about being informed of a team's lifetime record when they play on Tuesdays?

Forgive my rant. It's probably just jealousy.

I think, in many cases, the statistical overplay is a product of background. In their younger years, some play-by-play broadcasters worked alone. The only companion they could lean on was a batch of numbers. Numbers originally intended for backup, in case of a delay in proceedings, or maybe to fill for an AWOL intermission guest. Today though, with the expanded broadcast crews, statistical fill should be relegated to the recycle bin.

Total disclosure: I'm married to a beautiful young grandmother.

Sometimes Stuff Just Comes Out

THE COYOTES WERE IN Dallas one night, and the teams were tied in the third period. Colour commentator Tom Kurvers mentioned that on two similar occasions, Gerald Diduck had scored a late goal to give the Coyotes a win. With about a minute to go, it happened again, and here was the call: "Diduck scores! Diduck does Dallas...again!"

If you don't get it, ask your dad.

Rampant, Repugnant, "Homerism"

BACK IN THE DAY, being a "homer" was a no-no; now, it's rampant. Call me old school, but I can't stand when a broadcaster doubles as a cheerleader. It is something that has become more and more commonplace. Minnesota Vikings radio broadcasts are glorified pep rallies. Then there's Buck Martinez in Toronto. He has an infectious love of baseball and has great stories on both teams. Then he undermines his credibility by calling, "Outta here ball...get outta here!" when a Blue Jay hits a deep fly. It's hard to be objective when you're wearing pom poms.

I used to imagine someone far away tuning into a broadcast I was doing. I wanted him to have a hard time determining which team I was affiliated with. It's a show, of course, because if you work with a team, travel with a team, and attend their functions, you can't help but pull for them, but inwardly.

I remember Mike Haynes in Colorado. When the Avalanche scored, he'd lose it. When the opponent scored, he would drop to a whisper.

On the national front, "homerism" used to be discouraged, but it's not always the case anymore, particularly when it comes to Toronto Raptors telecasts.

You're the Boss

I SHOULD POINT OUT that some people are homers for a good reason; it's a condition of their employment. When Jack Kent Cooke owned the LA Kings, he insisted his team broadcasters always referred to their home rink as the "Fabulous Forum." And while it did look alright from the outside, the Forum was just another rink on the inside.

Jets President Barry Shenkarow once took exception to Friar and me saying that Mario Lemieux and the Pittsburgh Penguins were coming to Winnipeg. He felt any celebrity billing should be of a Jet.

Speaking of Mario Lemieux, when he announced his retirement as a player our TV host in Phoenix, Todd Walsh, did a fifteen-second tribute to him. Walsh was then chastised by Coyotes team President Doug Moss for saluting someone other than a Coyote. When Coyotes Owner and Coach Wayne Gretzky learned of it, he said, "Moss is a moron."

Shot in the Foot

WE USED TO DO an intermission promotion on CKY radio called the "$58,000 goal." A person would take one shot from the far blue line; if the puck entered the net through a small ice level slot, it was worth 58 grand. Some of the Jets tried at practice, and none could score; it seemed unlikely that anyone would.

However, we were wrong; the $58,000 goal was scored three times. Up until the last time, the radio station loved it. Every goal was great publicity and justified the expense of insuring it through Lloyd's of London.

Then in the final year, something totally unexpected happened. The late Ron Abel was emceeing the shot from ice level. A lady who looked like she had never seen a hockey stick before fanned on her shot, and the puck rolled about ten feet. In the eyes of the people watching, it was no shot at all. Abel knew otherwise; he knew a second shot would not be covered by insurance. So, what to do? Thousands of people were booing him. The promotion was backfiring! Abel was the station's all-important morning man. So, he made a spontaneous and seemingly very logical decision. He allowed the lady to take a second shot because there wasn't a chance she would even reach the net, let alone score.

So, what happened? Yes, a $58,000 uninsured goal!

Abel didn't sleep well that night.

Pride and Perceptions

MANY WON'T AGREE, BUT to me, unless you're saluting veterans or commemorating a special occurrence, flag-waving can be overkill. Pride in country is fine, but bragging often breeds resentment.

On the other hand, if you feel your country is getting a bad rap, it is time to speak up. Such was the case when America went to war with Iraq. There was a hockey game the next day in Montreal, and the American anthem was booed vociferously. It was headline material all over the US; it bothered me.

The Coyotes headed north the next day for a three-game trip through western Canada. On the flight, I approached our TV producer Jim Armintrout, and asked if we could break from the norm the next game and telecast the anthems. He said, "No. If I decide to carry the anthem and America gets booed, I could lose my job!" However, a while later, Armintrout relented. He said, "I can see this means a lot to you, so at great personal risk, we will carry the anthems tomorrow in Calgary." I said "great" and guaranteed him that America would be well received.

I can admit now that I was a little nervous waiting for the US anthem to end. What if I was wrong and didn't know my countrymen as well as I had promised I did? As it turned out, the people in the Saddledome gave the US anthem a prolonged standing ovation. My country was vindicated.

I was asked if we should do the same thing the next night in Edmonton and said "absolutely!" Again, we got a positive response. The trip concluded in Vancouver, and when asked the same question, I said, "Ah, no, maybe not here."

For the record, the response in Vancouver was polite applause.

Infantile

LARGE SCREENS ARE A big part of every pro sports facility, they enhance the goings on. In hockey, the screen is usually a part of the clock that overhangs centre ice. They'll show all kinds of videos and promotions, and they'll have the always popular crowd shots. They'll also have replays, and there's the rub.

In some buildings, the only goals you'll see replayed on the big screen are scored by the home team. They refuse to replay a visiting team's goal. It's as though they think if they ignore it, it'll go away. If you sit home and watch the game for nothing you get all kinds of looks. You can determine whether it was a great goal by the opponent, or a dunderhead play by the local. If you pay $100, forget it.

Of Friar, Witt, and Charlie

OVER MY TWENTY-SEVEN YEARS of broadcasting in the NHL, I had the good fortune to work with many outstanding people.

The best storyteller by a country mile was my first broadcast partner, the late Ken "Friar" Nicolson. Friar had a tremendous memory, and if it ever failed him, he had a gift for inventiveness. Friar was diabetic and in poor health. He suffered but never complained. When he was well enough to attend functions, he would always draw the largest crowd. People would gravitate to his table, and he would enamor them with humorous stories of his days traveling with the WHA Jets, or often about his days growing up in Thunder Bay.

He also liked to argue "on air." Thus, he and I did a lot of verbal sparring during broadcasts. He would get me worked into a lather then wink, and I'd realize I'd been set up (again). He may not have believed a word he was saying but got the reaction he wanted, and then he laughed. It was good radio.

I told each of my colour men after that to feel free to question anything I may say on the air, free to argue, but none did. It's funny, play-by-play people feel they have to agree with each other all the time, talk show hosts feel the need to disagree. The best for both is somewhere in between.

Friar was no hypocrite; if he liked you, you knew it and vice versa. He believed most people were worthy of respect; none was worthy of reverence. Armed with that philosophy, I became aware and embarrassed by a small but painfully obvious sycophantic element among NHL media.

I never met a man as bold as the late Don Wittman. "Witt" could walk into any situation like he owned the place. The fact that he was so widely recognized certainly helped, but I always had the impression that he was that way from the beginning. NHL dressing rooms were closed for ten minutes after a game, but that wasn't a problem for Witt. He'd simply line players up as they came off the ice and record them immediately. While those who followed protocol would still be waiting to enter the dressing room, he would be back in the press box with the interviews. On a given night, it would be Wayne Gretzky, Keith Tkachuk, and Teemu Selanne.

One night, in St. Louis, four of us decided to go to Busch Stadium to catch a Cardinals game. Coaches John Paddock and Andy Murray, along with Wittman and me. As we approached the ticket wicket, Wittman stopped me and said, "Sod, you and I don't buy tickets." As Paddock and Murray bought theirs, I said, "I thought we were going to the game too." Wittman laughed and said, "Follow me." He went directly to the Cardinals office and asked for General Manager Dal Maxvill. When told Maxvill was out of town, he slammed the desk and said, "Damn, he told me he'd be here and have a couple of tickets for me!" At that point, the receptionist called Maxvill's secretary. Wittman laid on the charm, and the next thing I knew, we had complimentary tickets and an apology. I then began walking toward our seats, and Wittman stopped me again and asked where I was going? I said, "To our seats, along the first baseline." "No," he said. "We don't sit there. We sit here, behind home plate, the best seats in the house." So, we did, but it didn't end there.

One deck above us we could see Paddock and Murray, so we laughed at them and sent a drink. To get us back, they sent security to check our tickets. Security approached me first, and my reply was "I defer to him," pointing at Wittman. I couldn't wait to hear how Don Wittman was going to wiggle out of this when suddenly the secretary we'd dealt with earlier stood up from just down the row and said, "No, no, leave them, they're GREAT friends of Mr. Maxvill!" (I doubt Witt had ever met him; I know I hadn't.)

It seemed everybody in Canada recognized Don Wittman. When he traveled with the Jets, he was often the most-watched person on the plane. I remember thinking that at one time, he was probably the second most recognizable person in the country (next to legendary TV news anchor Lloyd Robertson,) yet he was never paranoid and could not be embarrassed. He and I used to play cribbage on the commercial flights, and Witt was not a good loser. It was common for him to fling the cards in disgust and holler at me for being "so damn lucky." Our fellow passengers would then cover their faces to stifle a laugh. A minute later, Witt would gather the scattered cards, smile at the people, and want to play again.

A man who enjoys life is Charlie Simmer; he and I worked together in Phoenix. Charlie is a likeable sort who is known and respected by people in every NHL city; he seldom has anything negative to say. Charlie is also an organizer. If there was a day off on the road, Charlie would line up free golf, including clubs for anyone who wanted to come along. If it was too cold to golf, he'd line up a bowling alley or curling rink, and we'd pour out there and have a great time. Picking teams was never a problem. It was always the Canadians against the Americans because there was always a pretty even split.

Charlie is no longer directly involved with the NHL, which is a loss to the game. The former fifty-goal scorer was one of the game's great ambassadors.

The Bell Wouldn't Stop Ringing

ANOTHER OF MY FAVOURITE people came to be my broadcast partner because his head wasn't right. Coyotes defenceman Jimmy Johnson suffered three concussions in three weeks and missed only one game. The first concussion came in the '97 season opener when he took a big hit from Chicago Black Hawk Eric Daze. Over the next twenty days, he was concussed again and again. But in those days, concussions weren't taken seriously. Hockey people would simply say, "Jimmy got his bell rung; he'll be alright." But he wasn't, and it became all too apparent on Nov 11th, '97.

The Coyotes were playing at home against the Tampa Bay Lightning when Johnson got the puck at the point and instinctively let a shot go. He scored, but he didn't know it. The crowd began to cheer, and teammates mobbed him, but he was in the twilight zone; he had no idea what had happened. Sometime later, he confessed that he couldn't even see the net. Even the rink board advertising was all gobbledygook. Everything was swimming in his head, nothing seemed real, and nothing was in focus. After 829 games, he was playing on pure instinct. His goal came early in the second period, and he went on to finish the game. He played eighteen minutes that night and took twenty-four shifts. They would be the last shifts of his career. Johnson suffered constant headaches for three years, but fortunately, he is better now. He moved from the ice to the broadcast booth and ultimately to a coaching career.

As a broadcaster, Johnson was one of those who never really left the ice. Once during a playoff broadcast, when he felt Coyote Robert Reichel was avoiding contact, he hollered into the mic, "You can't play this game wearing a skirt!"

Dos and Don'ts

I OWE A LOT to my mentor, the late Ken "Friar" Nicolson. Friar was the voice of the Jets through the WHA years and into their early seasons in the NHL. I did colour commentary the first three NHL seasons, after which we traded positions due to Friar's failing eyesight.

Friar believed the public had the right to know, so if the Jets were playing poorly, he didn't hesitate to point it out. What was interesting about that was the reaction he would get. Coaches and players generally accepted the criticism, while the Jets ownership resented it.

Friar also taught me not to fraternize with the players. It can create jealousy and a lack of objectivity. You also may lose the trust of one of the most important people in your career, the team's head coach.

My late great friend, "Friar" Nicolson, could be cantankerous and charismatic at the same time.

Force-Feeding on the Fly

FRIAR NICOLSON WAS SUSCEPTIBLE to diabetic shock; it could come about at any time. On several occasions, it happened during a broadcast. His commentary would suddenly become slurred and wouldn't make any sense. The first half-sentence would be about a scoring chance, and the last half might refer to a tree in his backyard or a friend from high school. His voice would get higher, and there would be a lilt to it like he was singing. His delivery would get slow like an old 45 record, played at 33 speed. At that point, I would spring into action. I would have the operator shut off Friar's microphone and run to get a Coke or Pepsi. Then, it got tricky. I had to somehow pour soda into a reluctant throat. I'd grab him, force his mouth open and pour it in. How he didn't choke, I'll never know. Normally my "doctoring" would occur during a hastily called commercial break, but sometimes that wasn't possible, and I would find myself struggling to aim the coke while at the same time calling the play-by-play.

Two minutes later, the sugar would get to Friar's brain. We'd turn his mic back on and continue as though nothing had happened. And to Friar, nothing had happened; he would never remember any of it.

Who Are These People?

ONE TIME FRIAR AND I were calling a game, and Bruce Hood was the referee. I thought Hood was doing a good job, but Friar thought not. When Hood allowed a couple of minor infractions to go unpenalized, Friar said that Hood was in a big hurry to get the game over with. "He must have a date!" I got to know Bruce in later years when we worked together on television. I was anxious to have Hood and Friar meet so I could relate the story and make Friar squirm.

The three of us met for lunch in Toronto. The Harbour Castle Hotel dining room was set up with white table cloths; there were a lot of Bay Street types there, all decked out in their finest business attire. Friar and Hood shook hands, smiled, and all appeared well. Then suddenly, the slurring started. Friar was going into shock. I stood up in the packed dining room and hollered, "Get me a coke, NOW!" Hood had no idea what was going on; he sat with a glazed look, everyone in the dining room stared. It was serious but comical. So, I decided to wait before explaining. By the time the beverage came, Friar was totally incoherent, and I had to be aggressive, again. Now Hood was totally stupefied, and he wasn't alone. One of the business people yelled at me, "Unhand that man!"

I did get the coke into him, and after two minutes, we were all able to enjoy a good lunch and some laughs, and yes, the quizzical stares continued, which made it all the better.

The Shoe Is on the Other Foot

ON A COMMERCIAL FLIGHT back to Winnipeg, some of the WHA Jets thought they could get a good laugh at Friar's expense. They took his shoes while he slept and patiently awaited his reaction. However, when Friar awoke, he didn't react at all. He simply got off the plane in his socks as if nothing had happened. He then had his wife Margaret drive him directly to an exclusive shoe store where he ordered the most expensive shoes in the place, and had the bill sent to the Jets. The players had to pony up at practice a few days later.

Acceptance Leads to Enjoyment

IF A TEAM HAS a night off on the road, the "squatter's" rule takes effect. If a coach walks into a bar and there are players there, the coach is obliged to move elsewhere. On the other hand, if the coaches are there first, the players scatter in a heartbeat.

I spent a lot of those evenings with the coaches and thoroughly enjoyed them. Everything was wide open. I got to see the game through their eyes. I'd hear all kinds of stories and become aware of the real reason a particular player didn't dress for the last game. It wasn't always the "flu," as had been reported.

Gaining the trust of the coach was extremely important to me. It was easy with Tom Watt, Barry Long, Rick Bowness, John Paddock, Terry Simpson, Don Hay, Bobby Francis, and Wayne Gretzky, impossible with Tom McVie, tough with Jim Schoenfeld, strange with Bob Murdoch, and had to be earned with Dan Maloney.

Tough Made Easy

FROM A WORKING PERSPECTIVE, the biggest difference between the NHL of today and that of the mid-nineties and before is the travel. It's gone from a pain to a cakewalk.

In earlier times, every flight was commercial. If you travelled from Winnipeg, you could expect to spend huge irretrievable chunks of your life hanging around the Minneapolis Airport. Everybody hated it. In those days, a direct flight was as good as it got, and there were very few from Winnipeg.

On one occasion, the Jets went from Winnipeg to Anchorage, Alaska, for a preseason game, and even then, we went via Minneapolis. It took fourteen hours.

Nowadays, travel is the easiest part of the job; it's all charter. You can arrive at the airport a half-hour before the flight. There's a mandatory security check that takes only seconds, then board a luxury plane with all first-class seating. To add to it, there are fewer annoying announcements from the flight crew, and even their mandatory seat belt dance is cut short. It's the only way to fly and has lengthened the careers of many a coach, broadcaster, and equipment handler.

Space Cadet

WHEN YOU TRAVEL A lot, you can get disoriented. Yes, some of us more than others. I don't know how many times I woke up in a hotel room and took a while to figure what city I was in. Near the end of a four or five game trip, it was every morning.

One day though, I took it to another level. We were in Boston when I went to my room but couldn't get in. I went to the front desk and said, "I need a new key to room 854; this one doesn't work." The desk clerk said, "Well, there's a reason it doesn't work. This is the key to room 854 at the Westin, you're at the Marriot."

AWOL

A LOT OF HOCKEY people like to nap on a game-day afternoon. I could never do that, but I could "zone-out" for about five minutes. It was amazing how much better the brief respite would make me feel. Because it was so brief, I didn't need to arrange a wake-up call, or so I thought.

I got my comeuppance one day in the dead of winter. I woke up disoriented in a dark hotel room. My first thought was that it was early in the morning, and I should go back to sleep. Then I noticed I was dressed. Why? Where was I? What time is it? When everything came into focus, I realized I was in Ottawa and had a Coyote game due to start in an hour! In my life, I have never moved more quickly. I was cleaned, dressed, packed, and out the door in four minutes flat. I raced to a cab and was told we'd be at the rink in twenty minutes. He lied. To get to the Palladium from downtown Ottawa on a game night was an hour drive. When we finally got close to the rink, there wasn't time to go to the proper entrance. I hopped out of the cab and slid down a snowbank like Batman may have done with my suit bag in one hand and broadcast stuff in the other. I was in luck; the back door was open! When I entered, covered in snow, the first face I saw was Senator's broadcaster, Dean Brown. He read the situation immediately and while laughing, pointed to an elevator that took me straight to the press box. I hurried into the broadcast booth and grabbed my microphone in time to hear "on guard... for.... thee." Wow! Had there been only one anthem, I wouldn't have made it.

No Place Like Chicago

OLD CHICAGO STADIUM WAS a great place to broadcast hockey. The night would start with Wayne Messner's stirring renditions of the national anthems, accompanied by the incredible sound of a gigantic organ and a chorus of cheers. It charged the building with so much energy that halfway through the US anthem, you could barely hear the song. All the while, our suspended press box would shake. It was a totally different feel for someone who'd been raised to stand stoically during an anthem. At Chicago Stadium, the anthems were celebrated.

Chicago Stadium was in a notoriously bad part of town. Such that we always kept the postgame show as short as possible. If you missed the team bus back to the hotel, you might wind up staying until morning; taxis would not venture there after dark. We found that out the hard way one night but did manage at some personal expense to have one of the custodians take us back.

Even the Blackhawks players had to pay. They parked in an enclosed area, but if someone (rookie) refused to tip the lot attendant, his car would mysteriously suffer damage during the game.

Call Me a Fossil

I GREW UP WATCHING *Hockey Night in Canada* in black and white, so it was pretty exciting to go into an "original six" building for the first time. However, they were not always what I imagined. I recall the Jets maiden visit to Maple Leaf Gardens, the always candid Morris Lukowich skated over and said, "Wow, I dreamed of playing here, but this place is a dump!" In retrospect, it wasn't a dump; it was just drab. It was just a big, dull-looking building with a whole lot of seats and a painted ice surface. But really, what else did we expect? It's the way it was done back in the day. You'd pay a couple bucks for a seat, maybe fifty cents for a hot dog, have a cigarette, and enjoy the game. The kind of facilities they have now in places like Detroit, Edmonton, and Seattle, hadn't been imagined back then.

Hockey Shrine

GROWING UP WHERE I did, the only French anyone heard was spoken by Claude Mouton on Saturday nights: "La première étoile, Jean Beliveau." So, when I went to Montreal and heard that great PA voice again: "La première étoile, Guy Lafleur." It was déjà vu. The Montreal Forum was to hockey what Yankee Stadium was to baseball; it had an aura of greatness. There were larger-than-life displays of Rocket Richard, Doug Harvey, Jacques Plante, Dickie Moore, Toe Blake, Howie Morenz, and the list goes on. And that was just the lobby. The rink was adorned by twenty-three Stanley Cup banners (twenty-four now) and those names again on retired jerseys. The building seemed exactly as I'd seen it on black and white television decades earlier. It even had the checkered centre line that I believed was unique to the Forum. It was a "glorieux" step back.

In later years, the Forum was replaced by Bell Centre. One night I was calling a Coyotes game there and thought I could hear a familiar voice in the background. I looked around to see Danny Gallivan sitting alone in the booth next to me, practicing his play-by-play. The Legend was calling the game into his fist. I remember thinking, Wow! No wonder he's the best!

Dampened Enthusiasm

IT ISN'T EASY TO stretch a ring into a rink, but they did in Boston. The Boston Garden was built in 1928 primarily as a Boxing venue with the Bruins as an add-on, the Celtics came along eighteen years later. To accommodate hockey, they put in a smaller than normal ice surface. The close proximity of the boards led to more physical contact and spawned the "Big, Bad" Bruins.

The radio broadcast booth in Boston was an afterthought. To access it, you had to duck and enter through a "doggie" door. The location however was the best. It was so close to the ice you could hear the chatter and almost feel the hits. It was also immediately below a deck that facilitated the "Gallery Gods." These were blue-collar people who lived and died by the fortunes of their team. They were raucous when the Bruins were winning, subdued at other times. They also had a tendency to imbibe.

One night the Jets were doing well at the expense of the Bruins, and it wasn't sitting well with my overhead neighbours. During a commercial break, one bearded guy who was missing a tooth mocked my call of a Jet goal. Sometime later, the Jets scored again, and suddenly I was dripping wet. Yikes! But what a relief, my "golden shower" was only beer!

I guess he could read my thoughts because when I looked up at my dentally challenged friend, we both had a good laugh. I never had a problem again.

The Silenced Voice

I'M SOMETIMES ASKED WHY I no longer broadcast NHL hockey. Rather than go into all the gory details, I just say, "I'm retired." However, I can't exit this mortal coil without revealing the whole gruesome story.

It seems the Peter principle came into play because the people who orchestrated my demise both achieved their positions by default. Doug Moss became president of the Phoenix Coyotes after Brian Byrnes had declined the position, saying he wasn't ready. Byrnes chose to stay on as vice president. Moss' first act when he took over was to fire Byrnes. That paranoid display was indicative of the chaos that was to ensue through his entire reign.

The other perpetrator of my banishment was a TV executive, Mike Connelly. He became manager of the FOX satellite operation in Phoenix after producer Jim Armintrout turned down the promotion. Connelly's fervent anxiety to wield power was evident immediately, when he told acquaintances he was going to take the Coyotes off the air because Wayne Gretzky didn't say "Hi" to him at a function.

One day at the arena, some of the television people began to laugh over a text from Connelly. He reported that he was having lunch with Doug Moss, and the cowardly president was acquiescing to his every wish. Connelly added that he expected Moss to be under the table "servicing him" at any minute. Months later I learned that the conversation had been about me. Connelly wanted me gone. (He needed the rush, I guess?)

While this was happening, I was negotiating a new contract. The Coyotes told my representative that they were "thrilled" by my work and that a new deal was imminent. I could not have been happier. Thus, it came as a total shock when I arrived bright-eyed at Moss' office on May 4th, 2007, and was told I was done! The Coyotes were going in a "different direction."

It made no sense at all. To add to the absurdity, Moss was quoted in the local newspapers as saying, "Curt did a great, great job and wonderful things in the community, but we've decided to go in a different direction." Huh?

In retrospect, nothing should have surprised me. In 2004 when the NHL lockout appeared unavoidable, I asked Moss what compensation I could expect in a worst-case scenario. He told me I would receive half my salary. I thanked him. In mid-August of that year, there was no paycheque. I called Moss to ask what happened, and he broke into song, "No play...no pay...ha ha."

Moss had become president on the recommendation of his friend Gary Bettman. Thus, when the Coyotes got into financial trouble and rumours began circulating that they would return to Winnipeg, Bettman was seen on television praising Moss for keeping things together during a time of turmoil. So, it was interesting that when the league took over the franchise and got an up-close look at what was really going on, the first thing they did was fire Bettman's buddy.

There was a final shattering experience a few years after Moss was tossed. The Coyotes were back in the market for a play-by-play TV broadcaster and wanted me to return. I excitedly told them I would. Connelly heard about it, and even though he was leaving Arizona, said, "If you hire him, I'll take the Coyotes off the air!"

And as often happens at Day Care, petulance prevailed.

Petrified Moss

I DID GET ONE brief moment of immense satisfaction four months later. The Coyotes played a preseason game in Winnipeg, and much to my surprise, President Moss made the trip. I could not have lived with myself if I'd passed on the opportunity to vent.

Shortly after the game, we came face-to-face with no one else around. I looked him in the eye and the whole speech I had planned drifted away. Instead, a deep-throated insult spewed out of me, followed by an insane cackle. It was eerie; I sounded like something out of a horror show. I scared him to the point that he began to blubber. That's how I learned of Mike Connelly's involvement. He then staggered away with his hand over his chest. I thought he might collapse. I won't say how I felt about that.

Freddy Didn't Say "Friggin'"

SOMETIMES, WE IN THE media can be a little too inquisitive, even invasive in the eyes of a particular hockey player on a particular night.

The highest scoring defenceman in the history of the original NHL Jets was a tall Swede, Freddy Olausson. Freddy didn't try to be different; he just was. On team flights, when others were playing cards or reading John Grisham, Freddy was reading Donald Duck. He's what people now would call a free spirit or a flake. Others just referred to him as "Freddy the Fog," you never quite knew where his head was.

One thing you couldn't question though, was his talent. He was an outstanding skater with a booming shot. He was a natural on the power play. Winnipeg people recognized his ability, but some questioned his effort. They booed him.

So it came to pass that early one season, Freddy was firing on all cylinders. His passes were on the tape; his shots were on the net. He was becoming more popular but still not the fan favourite. Twenty games in, Freddy was leading the Jets in scoring. One night in November, he was dominant. He scored two goals and was the best player on the ice in a game the Jets lost.

He was named the second star and spoke to our three-man broadcast crew from ice level. I started the questioning and asked how it felt personally to be leading the team in scoring? His answer: "Not very good, we lost the game."

Don Wittman picked up the questioning from there. "No Freddy, it's got to feel great to you personally to be leading the team in scoring in light of the way the fans have reacted to you."

Olausson again said, "No, it doesn't feel good; we lost the game."

At that point, Ted Irvine chimed in, "Ah come on Freddy you're on fire, you're having a career year, tell us how you really feel!"

Freddy's clear, concise answer to a radio audience of several thousand, "Just friggin' wonderful."

Only, Freddy didn't say "friggin.'"

Thanks for taking the time to read my book. I hope you found something you enjoyed.

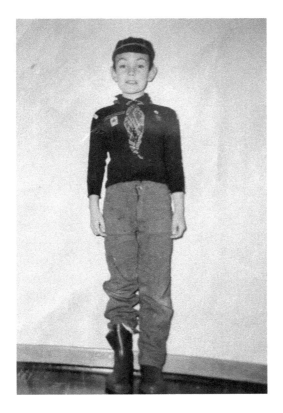

My ma always said,
"To be sharp, you've got to look sharp."

CPSIA information can be obtained
at www.ICGtesting.com
Printed in the USA
LVHW112159230922
729165LV00002B/62

9 781039 146006